It's Not That Deep

It's Not That Deep

The Essential Workbook
for Simplifying Your Life
as a Tattoo Artist

Jack Ede

Copyright © 2025 Jack Ede
All rights reserved.

It's Not That Deep
The Essential Workbook for Simplifying Your Life as a Tattoo Artist

First Edition

ISBN 978-1-5445-4655-1 *Hardcover*
     978-1-5445-4654-4 *Paperback*
     978-1-5445-4656-8 *Ebook*
     978-1-5445-4657-5 *Audiobook*

Contents

Introduction 9
1. What Do You Truly Want? 15
2. How Much Do You Want It? 19
3. Suffering and Destructive Behaviour 25
4. Education and Apprenticeships 33
5. Stay True to YOU 45
6. Beware of the Vampires 53
7. A Little Validation 61
8. The Craft 67
9. The Pursuit of Originality 77
10. Practice and Patience 83
11. The Business: The Blind Leading the Blind 97
12. Our Dear Clients 109
13. The Chain of Influence 117
14. Money, Money, Money 127
15. Amateur to Professional 141
    Acknowledgments 147
    About the Author 149

Introduction

The amount of times I drew on my hands and arms as a kid, you'd think I was dying to become a tattoo artist. But if you asked me back then, I'd have no idea what you're talking about; I was just drawing.

It wasn't until I quit high school that I actually considered making real tattoos. I was obsessed with making realistic art, and so my main focus was to make the best possible pencil drawings and nothing else. Because of my success with that, I was shared via Instagram's official page in late 2014, resulting in approximately sixty thousand new followers in the first three days. Due to the overwhelming surge of attention, I was offered a handful of apprenticeships.

Considering how tough it was to maintain a steady income through producing and selling my drawings, I figured I could throw tattooing into the equation and juggle it all. I was just shy of my nineteenth birthday when I flew from England to Denmark to begin my tattoo apprenticeship. The initial plan was to study there for a couple of months until the studio opened their new branch in London. Everything was so exciting: being surrounded by big personalities, planning the future, and feeling seen was everything I craved.

At the time, I was anaesthetised with false hope and empty promises of stability and comfort. What I experienced was closer to the opposite. I like to believe my employers meant well, but we all bonded through our excess ambition, confidence, and "fuck the system" approach to life and business. As a result, we all suffered immensely due to our combined lack of literally everything else that we actually needed to run a business.

Despite being hired as an employee, only a mere two to three months into my journey, I was personally asked to lend my bosses money to pay for a variety of large expenses throughout the construction process. Nothing looked like the pictures they painted, and the red flags started to pop up behind each door.

For the first six months, I spent every waking moment in what was nothing more than a poorly renovated three-storey shithole with tacky furniture, a few broken windows, and my belly full of £1 pizzas.

I made hundreds of tattoos during this period, and I was unattended during 99 percent of them. I was advised to watch over people's shoulders, ask questions, or figure shit out by myself, but that only made me feel like a burden to everyone. It wasn't until my buddy CB joined us and offered a shoulder to lean on that I received any kind of technical guidance. He was the closest I had to a mentor, and everything he offered was through the kindness of his heart.

We had a beautiful summer in London that year, so the front door was always open. I remember a guy came in piss drunk, asking if we could rework an old dragon tattoo on his back. At that time, I was one of the only artists available, and most of us weren't feeling it. The guy was difficult to deal with, and we were ill-prepared and underqualified. The man in charge caught wind that we didn't take the drunk's money, and things turned sour.

The clients were asked to step outside so he could have a quiet word with us all. Naturally, this six foot four coke fiend was quick to anger. *"If you don't fancy making money, then i suggest you find somewhere else to fuck about"*. His north London vocals bounced around this rickety townhouse. Fear entered the chat, and I'm fairly confident someone pissed themselves. Could've been me. Specifics don't matter here.

Bear in mind, this man had barely paid any of us in the six months prior. Half the cash went in his pocket and later disappeared through his nasal cavities. To insult us further, he demanded we pay an extortionate amount of rent. I suppose he thought cash grew from our arses.

The last thing I remember was CB and I packing our belongings and heading an hour south to his parents' place. Yep, I definitely pissed myself.

Eventually, I ziplined home so I could recharge. You'd think I'd have learnt from that experience, but my hungry heart was lured in for round two only a few months later.

In my absence, the London branch had fallen apart, and so I returned to Denmark. With a brand-new suitcase filled with hope and broken biscuits, I arrived fully convinced that I'd begin living the reality I was promised. It was certainly an improvement—this time I had a less broken window in my bedroom above the studio.

In the following five years, I merely survived at that place, putting my heart into every tattoo with the odd trip back home. I experienced brief moments of joy with equal parts of sadness. I'd make a drawing every few months, but I found more comfort in smoking.

I've always worked for the same kind of people in the same kind of places. It was only after I'd suffered enough that I decided to draw the line.

In 2022, I snapped out of it. I was beaten and bruised, and my path of destruction was haunting me. I was Liam Neeson, the intricacies of my mind were the bad guys, and my inner peace was the kidnapped daughter. I spent the year sharpening my particular set of skills. I expected it to be like killing bad guys, but in reality, it was like being on a roller coaster designed by a meth-head.

In 2023, I had cleaned up the majority of the mess, and Liam Neeson's daughter (my inner peace) had returned. I finally started to walk the walk and notice my values align. I managed to redefine my own system as an artist, making tattoos privately, making and selling paintings that excited me, and tutoring others who didn't have a mentor, all with plenty of rest in between, financial peace of mind, and a greater overview of my health than I ever dreamed possible.

As I write this story, it's been around fifteen months without turbulence. I've never been so consistently creative, happy, healthy, well rested, and in love with every moment (even the tough ones). On top of that, I've built a relationship with myself where there's no surprises. I finally feel like I'm driving my own ship, and my headlights are incredible. As a self-employed artist, I'm able to control my workload, meaning I can offer my clientele and the people in my life 100 percent of me always, with plenty of extra time to adjust.

Going from someone who was constantly drained, unstable, broke, and struggling to commit to anything to someone who was drawing and painting almost every day, tattooing an average of three days a week, and earning five figures a month at a gentle pace, as well as writing, publishing, and funding their very own book—this is beyond the transformation I ever dreamed of.

My goal was never to achieve all those things; it was simply to combat the dysfunction in my mind. Only by doing so did it become clear that a healthy foundation and a realistic mindset could help me attain anything, despite all the shit I was led to believe during the prior eight years.

I wrote this book because:

1. I physically can't keep my mouth shut when I care.
2. I also hate listening to people preach, so I figured I'd let you read my story yourselves.

The biggest thing I've learnt along my journey is that, as humans, we're truly fucking annoying. We're desperate for helpful knowledge, but if it comes from someone else telling us, we will literally refuse to take it. We must stumble upon it ourselves countless times until we learn. And when we do, we will rise from the ashes practising what we preach, claiming we knew that shit all along.

I truly hope you find something useful in this book; may it release you from your tethers and guide you home.

Topic #1

What Do You Truly Want?

Many of us get led astray, distracted by shiny things, in our pursuit of a life idealised by others, praying for delivery to a place of peace and harmony. We're so influenced by our surroundings that we can't tell which thoughts and feelings are even ours.

Some of us grew up being the weird ADHD kid who drew a lot and barked at people. We believed that we were destined for failure before we even had a chance to stretch our legs.

> I suppose our teachers were right about us being destined for failure, since we're still here figuring shit out, thriving in depression, and masking our every move whilst simultaneously riddled with trust issues and an insatiable hunger for improvement.

Life's gonna move fast for as long as you let it, and the longer you do, the longer your teacher was right.

I know you're probably thinking, "Damn, get to the point already", and to that I say, "Patience, my child".

In a nutshell, if you don't have a clear view of where you'd like to go, it's possible you'll encounter a demon who will guide you.

> **Early disclaimer:** You don't *have* to know yet, but you are prey for clever business fellas who need impressionable little worker bees, so it could help to ask yourself to decide.

If you're already neck deep in the industry with your own studio, kids, and a dog, then you can probably skip this part. (Unless you low-key hate your life. Then hello and welcome.)

If you're somewhere in between, and you feel like you're at a crossroads with your career, you're in the right place.

And if it's your very first day here, buckle up, sunshine.

TATTOOIST OR TATTOO ARTIST?

In the industry, we have two main types of people:

1. We have the "tattooists" who mostly enjoy the lifestyle and the idea of tattooing. They work for money and keep things simple. Often the extroverted type.
2. Then we have the "tattoo artists" who make tattoos as another form of creation and expression. These are the sensitive, introverted type who suffer the most, for they simply live to create.

Of course, there are—and will always be—people who bounce between both extremes.

Now it's time to look in the mirror.

If you happen to resonate with a particular statement below, it'll make your internal navigation a little easier.

1. Tattooing is everything to me. I want to do it for the rest of my life. I love the community, and I understand I'm part of something bigger than myself. I'm grateful I can support my lifestyle with it.
2. Tattooing is great. It's a cool job and a great way to make money. I can travel wherever I want and have a good time.
3. I enjoy tattooing. It's another form of expression for me. I'm grateful for all encounters with new people. I don't rely on the income. I aim to make tattoos and live life this way for as long as I can.
4. I've never thought about why I make tattoos, I just like the idea of it.

If none of these sound like you, perhaps try to write your own before diving into the rest of the book.

VISUALISATION QUESTIONS

For a long time, I was driven by money and pleasing others because I believed it would take me to where I wanted to go. The result: I constantly suffered.

I've presented a few questions that will feel like an internal tug of war. There is no right answer; the point is to kick-start a healthy conversation with yourself in the hope that your priorities will become clear.

Perhaps you're so used to prioritising others that you forget you even have a choice.

1. It's official—the zombies will be here tomorrow. It's your last chance to make a sick tat. What do you make? (One hundred percent chance of infection, obviously.)
2. Side quest—your boss asks you to tattoo on a Sunday. You'll make some extra cash, but you'll lose a day of rest. Will you go?
3. If money wasn't part of the equation, would you still make tattoos?
4. Your crush wants one of your flash designs, but they don't have any money. What do you do?

The main idea of this section is to get you familiar with your sense of self and to curate a realistic path forward.

You don't have to fully believe it yet, but it would help to invest a little time laying your foundation before you return to the battlefield.

And by battlefield, I literally mean the tattoo studio. It's a fair comparison, in my opinion.

Topic #2

How Much Do You Want It?

This is a huge grey area in the industry; everyone has their own ideas of how much we should put up with and how serious we need to be.

It's rare that you're asked, "How serious do you wish to take your job?" so you automatically assume you're supposed to go all in.

Of course, it can't all be sunshine and rainbows. In some cases, we must compromise for the better cause, and the sooner we accept this, the sooner we can enjoy the entire spectrum of possibilities.

However, balance is key and *you're* responsible for finding out how to balance your own life, no one else.

When you first contact a studio for work, you're only introduced to their facade, and you proceed blindly until you gain experience with your new reality.

Soon enough, you're familiar with the setup and you're convinced you can make it work. Even if your gut sends you signals, you'll be advised to give it a chance. You may see it as a challenge and invest even more energy into it.

The conflicts begin when you get comfortable with your peers and start discussing your goals.

Just because others have big dreams for themselves, doesn't automatically mean you should have some, too, and vice versa.

You've probably heard the saying, "If you're not building your own dream, you're helping someone else build theirs", which is totally fine if you're aware of that and all your needs are met, but that is not always the case.

There's a fine line between having small goals and being considered unambitious, and modern-day people typically wish to avoid unambitious people.

There's also a fine line between having big goals and being overly confident and unrealistic, and this type does not typically mix with the chill type.

In a work environment, there's rarely space for people to have separate ambitions without being influenced by one another.

The moment you feel less/more than your peers, you tend to subconsciously adapt or avoid.

Adapting without awareness can lead you towards making poor choices for *you*.

Avoiding can result in scenarios causing all to suffer.

We're either too honest or we just say whatever sounds the best to protect ourselves from momentary rejection and discomfort.

Yet we only manage to tolerate and never fully accept one another as we are.

What started as a simple wish to work in a tattoo shop could be twisted into a complete ambush of your best efforts.

PRACTISE WHAT YOU PREACH

Now, you always have options; you can adapt or avoid, but you cannot control anyone else (ethically, of course, stay focused).

The only factor you *can* control is how *you* act each and every step of the way.

This is why having a general idea of what you wish to *attract* in life is very helpful.

My theory is that the more you reflect and honour your own values, the less turbulence you'll experience, and the less harm you'll inflict on others around you.

> **Please note:** If you're just beginning your journey, it's a lot easier to create a healthy relationship with yourself now than it will be as the years go by.

Below is a system I've created that could help you make sense of a situation just a wee bit quicker. The goal with it is to establish whether something is genuinely what *you* want to do, or whether it's something you are *influenced* to do. This could be a tattoo project, a career change, a personal identity crisis, or simply learning how to say no to a dinner invitation.

Let's say you've just finished a five-day work week. It's 10.00 p.m. on a Friday. You're smashed and ready to destroy a pint of ice cream in front of your favourite series.

You get a cheeky notification on your phone, and to your disgust, it's not Tinder; it's YOUR BOSS! He needs you to tattoo his friend for a good price this weekend.

Before you respond, give yourself a moment to consider your options.

Subject: Tattooing this weekend

- Is this a priority at the moment?
- Will this benefit me/my family/my team?
- Will this *give* me energy?
- Will this *cost* me energy?
- Will this affect my focus on the bigger picture?
- Will this cause an imbalance in my life?
- Do I have a choice?
- Do I care what others think?
- Am I influenced or pressured by my boss/peers?
- Is there a financial incentive/gain?
- If so, do I need it more than I need rest?
- Am I afraid of the outcome not going my way?

Now this is just step one. Step two is respecting yourself enough to follow through on your final outcome without bullshitting yourself.

After doing that enough times, you'll begin to have a solid bond with yourself and your peers because they, too, will see you respect yourself and will know where you stand.

Assuming that you're already sure of which lifestyle you have, or would *like* to have, this part should be fairly simple. If not, give it a try anyway.

The ultimate benefit of this exercise is that you'll strengthen your conviction for your career and respect for your own values. This will especially benefit you in those crucial moments when you're put on the spot, and you don't know what to say.

The result will be finding yourself in more harmonious situations, favouring balance and value for all.

TIME TO SUPPORT YOURSELF

To truly support oneself is to accept, love, and forgive unconditionally—not only yourself, but everyone and everything you encounter. To have patience and compassion, especially on the bad days. To reason with oneself and come to mutual agreements with one's ego.

Imagine you simply accept yourself as you are each day. You don't even look in the mirror because you know you'll never be perfect. You do the best you can, knowing that doing what you love is a privilege. You avoid using harmful language with yourself. You respect and value your rest days, as you know they serve you well.

Each day is a fresh opportunity to live well, to say, "Hi" to strangers, and make lives easier for those around you. To make crisper lines, pack your colours better, and watch your clients smile. To move more, drink more water, and love yourself a little more. You don't have to seize the opportunity, but isn't that what you want?

Before you know it, you're feeling better in your own mind, and you vaguely recall the last period of turbulence. FOMO grows weaker by the day, and now *you* decide when you say yes. You're no longer bothering yourself to hurry up, pressuring yourself to improve. You're moving at your own natural rhythm, balanced, rested, positive, and supportive of yourself.

This may sound ridiculous to some of you, and I completely understand. I felt the same before I truly supported myself, and I certainly never believed it would compound into even more peace and clarity as I continued.

I don't make a lot of promises, but I am beyond confident that it feels better than following the crowd. Better than going out every weekend or accepting every single social invitation, even though you're still recovering from the last.

It *is* possible to support *you*.

Topic #3

Suffering and Destructive Behaviour

In my time within the industry, I have encountered many special characters. Some became great friends—others, parasites. A few genuine souls in the *wrong* place, and a handful of genuine souls in the *right* place, just at the wrong time.

I eventually met this one guy, a very confused soul indeed. He seemed like a decent friend, yet he held me back more than anyone.

Whenever I'd try to commit to something, he'd interfere. Happy making art? He'd show me something better to do. Countless times he'd blame everyone else for hindering my progress.

He'd make my life hell for never doing enough each day, and he actually thought that would motivate me. I know, right? A difficult fella indeed.

Funny story, though: he's actually the author of this book.

"I thought being a tattoo artist was a cool and chill career."

It can be. This is just how I experienced it, because I was

in pain, and so was everyone else. In hindsight, it's impressive that we never OD'd from our own self-pity.

At the beginning, I leant on people who told me they knew the way, only to be led to a place less familiar.

I resented poor advice and developed ill habits to cope with stress. I felt like no one was capable of helping me because they didn't live the life I *felt I* deserved. They didn't "walk the walk".

Deep down, I knew I was the only one who could help me; I just refused to believe it.

I tell you this because I believe in order to successfully help *ourselves*, we must first address the dysfunction *within* ourselves. We're so familiar with blaming others, the weather, or any other external happenings for our misery, that we never dare to consider it's been us the entire time.

So, if you fancy it, ask yourself these questions:

- If I talked to my friends the way I talk to myself, would they be okay with it?
- Do I have any unresolved emotions that could be affecting me?
- Do I self-medicate with short-term fixes such as cigarettes, drugs, alcohol, social media, and/or other addictive substances?
- Do I distract myself or constantly make plans to avoid being alone?
- Do I refuse to accept my current reality and constantly chase a better future?
- Do I blame, reject, or avoid others who don't fit the image of my desires?

If this is an entirely new language to you, then I encourage you to take it at your own pace.

If it's something you really struggle with, then it could be worth speaking to a professional to support you.

It took me years to speak to a therapist, and it was by far the greatest act of value I've done for myself.

I know, I know. This book isn't supposed to be a testimony for therapy and healing. But, I mean, it kinda is.

I love that I care so much, and I want you to feel good as well.

I want our clients to *genuinely* be in safe hands.

I dream that we all drop the act and take responsibility for ourselves.

All you posers and tough guys out there, I beg you to help yourselves and clean up your work stations, literally and metaphorically. You have so much value to share, and we need your love as well.

Fun fact: Did you know that smoking a pack of cigarettes every day is not helping with your stress?

THERE IS NO PEACE WITHOUT SUFFERING

I'd like to discuss the nature in which we tend to address suffering.

I know it sounds barbaric—and perhaps a little dramatic—for a book about tattooing. But in my nine years of experience, I honestly can't remember a single soul who didn't suffer.

Sure, suffering is a part of who we've been, who we are, and who we will always be.

Yet, until we finish chewing what we already have in our mouths, perhaps we should stop biting off more and more every day.

We fight fire with fire and wonder why it never dies.

Every artist I've known has suffered in their own unique way, whether it was past or still present, and they didn't realise that they continued to inflict harm on themselves as a coping mechanism.

It's tricky because we're still the children of a generation that was taught to be tough. And if you ain't tough, you gotta act tough. Luckily, half of us are terrible actors, and the other half are great at reading between the lines; we just need to get better at cooperating.

I'd like to explore some real-life scenarios where we can observe our own mental state and those of our peers. Imagine you're listening to your friend complaining one morning in the prep room. (Nothing new, sadly.)

They can't believe their ex left them, and now he's liking their pictures again (the audacity!!).

Sure, you want them to feel better, but perhaps you dissociated ten minutes ago, and really, you just want them to shut the fuck up.

It's not even tattoo related, but they're your friend, and you work together. So, naturally, you're obligated to listen, right?

Wrong.

There's a time and a place, and it's not the prep room. Especially when you both have work to do.

Naturally, you wanna blame them. I get it.

Perhaps you think, "Why do I always get stuck listening to complete nonsense? I never ask for it."

Or "I guess I'm just so empathetic, they love opening up to me."

Truth is, you could both do better. You just have a little work to do and could both benefit from an honest one-to-one chat.

HOW TO OPEN A TOUGH DISCUSSION

It can be especially tough if neither of you recognizes your dysfunction, let alone take responsibility for it. But let's use our imagination for a second.

On this particular day, you're aware of the lack of boundaries, and you desperately wish to avoid interactions like this, especially in the workplace when you have a client. It's tough for you to say it in person, so naturally, you text "bro" when you get home.

"Hey bro, I just wanted to talk about
something that's been bugging me a little."

"What's up bitch??"

"Ha ha. Basically, sometimes when we're at
the studio and you mention some random
shit, I find it super difficult to get
my focus back and it affects my work."

"Ah okay, my bad, I guess I just
thought it was funny or something"

"Well yea sometimes it's funny, but
shouldn't our priority be to focus
on why we're actually there (making
tats), and then we can talk about
our private issues afterwards?"

"Ur right, I guess I just got too
comfortable cuz ur my bro etc"

"I feel that, I just wanted to talk
about it because I care about us
both and want us to do well."

"*insert homophobic insult which is
totally not funny or appropriate ever and
which I completely do not support btw*"

"Just kidding bro, I appreciate
u reaching out."

"Of course. But if you do ever need to
talk about something that's difficult or
unrelated to tattooing, I'm always here."

"Likewise dude, thanks for
bringing it up. I'll do better."

In your own environment, do interactions like this happen?

If so, do you have anxiety about communicating? Do you feel resentment growing? Do others feel it too?

Does the idea of setting boundaries between you and your colleagues seem uncomfortable?

Is it necessary to do so?

If you value your own mental clarity and appreciate your opportunity, your client, your fellow peers, and the craft you're paid to do, then the answer should be, "Yes, I need to set boundaries".

The other option is to continue suffering and feeding your own destructive behaviour, as well as your colleague's.

If you're the first to notice some room for improvement, and it doesn't seem likely that your friend will act first, then do the noble deed and step up.

Again, this is just a simple workplace scenario. It is one that I've personally endured hundreds of times, and one that I've created hundreds of times.

I never had the strength to step in and set my own boundaries.

I never even knew what boundaries were, and neither did the others.

I could've saved myself hours and hours of frustration.

I could've saved my colleagues and friends hours and hours of frustration.

I could've given more energy and enthusiasm to my clients, resulting in a better tattoo.

I could've had better relationships with people, instead of resenting/avoiding our unnecessary workplace interactions.

I could've...

But I didn't.

And so I suffered.

> **Side note:** Blocking the world out and focusing on yourself may feel like a good idea at the time. However, you're still avoiding a responsibility, and it will come back to bite you in the ass. Sorry.

These minor interactions became toxic little tumours in my mind, body, and soul. All because I never learnt to speak up and set boundaries.

My focus and passion was tattooing, yet half of my days were spent fighting for my sanity.

This wasn't in the contract! Where are the adults?

Are there any?

Or is everyone still suffering because we weren't taught how to act around each other?

We do not have to accept this or normalise this behaviour.

Take responsibility. Start the conversation.

Topic #4

Education and Apprenticeships

To this very day I'm still frequently baffled by the puzzles presented to me when I make a tattoo or when working with my peers and clients. Sometimes it feels like not one single element in the process is cohesive. We do not stand a chance at controlling all the variables involved.

Is it my state of mind? Is it actually the needles that are shit? Do I simply need a new machine? Maybe it's the music. What about my client? Are they in on this sick joke that's making my life hell today? I bet someone's recording this shit for content.

It's become clear to me that the only variables we can master are the ones we're personally responsible for, and everything else must be met with grace.

I'm sure you've tattooed whilst hungover before and made the cleanest tattoos you've ever done. You were probably so focused on feeling like death that your natural abilities took over and made that shit look easy.

I'm sure you've tattooed your favourite designs, where you're well rested, happy as Larry, yet nothing's going your way, and you're telling yourself you're the worst tattooist there is.

Truth is, it was less about your natural abilities and more about your mentality the entire time.

When the variables are positive, we tend to try extra hard to make this the best tattoo we've ever made, resulting in us stressing and making hot trash.

When the variables are not so positive, we tend to focus on just getting through the day, passively accepting that we'll do our best and expect nothing more, and usually the result is surprising.

However, this is where we start to misinterpret "trying too hard" and "not trying at all".

THE TATTOO APPRENTICESHIP

I can't speak for how it used to be, but the fact we're still making tattoos for a living implies that the old schoolers must've done something right. Sure, their strategies were likely human rights violations and would easily break today's generation, but it worked.

Similar to being a cadet in the army, you'd suffer, you'd starve, you'd cry, you'd sleep wherever you could, you'd see lifeless bodies on a daily basis, you'd smoke way too many cigarettes, and your sex life would cease to exist (or you'd pay for it). Honestly, you'd likely wish you were never born. But despite all that, at least you'd become a solid tattooer.

> **Bonus gift:** 100 percent PTSD guarantee upon completion! Terms and conditions may apply.

Nowadays, most people suffer this very same way, all for the love of tattooing and a colourful life. Yet there's no actual guarantee they will become a good tattoo artist.

In the past nine years, I've witnessed an unsettling number of half-assed apprenticeships, including my own. I've also seen some traditionally successful ones that appeared to have worked until the artist went their own way, only to reveal a weak foundation. I believe both parties are equally responsible for the low success rate, but not as much as the general lack of conviction by the industry as a whole.

The entire educational system is completely unreliable. Or rather, there simply isn't one and it's all a mirage. There are no official standards anywhere, no certification process, no legitimately qualified teachers, and no one to regulate or hold people accountable.

Hygiene is being traded out for whatever is quickest, easiest, or looks coolest, so if your client dies, it's likely your fault and not because they drank four beers. Unless you teach yourself entirely from scratch (please don't), the shop owner or your "master" will likely control your fate.

Your first studio is where you learn to walk, and if they tell you hopping on one leg is more efficient, you'll likely believe them.

The lack of professionalism overall is what leaves holes for child's play, so the majority of our efforts are spent processing drama, emotional manipulation, and amateur mind games.

I spent most of my time as an apprentice wondering how to communicate and impress my peers, all whilst simultaneously navigating through depression with my trusty copilot, "Mr Anxiety".

I never had an official "master", so I was advised to learn whatever I could from anyone who'd offer a moment of their time. Luckily for me, I learn pretty well just by observing, but this isn't the case for a lot of people.

The fact that most people were so unpredictable and dysfunctional, including myself, made this method a complete nightmare. Hence why the majority of my efforts were spent on communication and survival, and tattooing came in last.

THE TEACHER

Teaching the craft has become more of a business strategy than a genuine love for making tattoos.

Everyone knows that good teachers are the ones who truly love the subject they're teaching.

Modern-day studios will hire apprentices for a multitude of reasons. Rarely do any of them involve a genuine passion for tattooing.

The reasons for this include:

- They have no choice.
- They can't say no.
- Superiority complex.
- Passive income.
- The "master" status.
- The dream of early retirement.
- Someone's pregnant.
- Trying to save the marriage (business) by having a child (apprentice).
- All of the above.

Now, since people are free to do whatever they please, it's rude to suggest that it's wrong.

However, if you don't commit to giving the person a solid education, then that's exactly what I'm suggesting.

If you do follow through, and the person doesn't end up completely traumatised, then congratulations!

Nonetheless, it doesn't really matter why you take them on to begin with, as long as they get what they signed up for.

I like to say, "If you're doing your best, yet you continue to fail miserably and continue to make others feel uncomfortable and frustrated, then please stop charging money for it". This applies to both students and teachers.

Taking on an apprentice for the wrong reasons is like watching someone get a dog to cure their own depression, and then the dog ends up depressed too.

As a teacher, you have a huge responsibility. It's not something you can only juggle when you have the energy and still claim all the benefits.

If you have no interest in truly educating someone, then why pretend to? Why would you waste everyone's time, including your own?

If you still communicate poorly with yourself and others around you, why would you take responsibility for teaching someone who's vulnerable?

Do you think teaching someone else is your shot at redemption? Will it erase your failed apprenticeship so you don't have to rebuild your foundations?

There's no such thing as a perfect teacher, but please don't bite off more than you can chew.

If they're willing to give it 100 percent, then you need to as well.

If you can't do better, why not be honest and let your student find someone better suited for the job?

I BLAME THE RAT RACE

I'm sure other countries have successful methods for apprenticeships. They just haven't reached mainland Europe or the US yet.

Usually, people excel as students because of the countries' overall values and beliefs, pressure from their environment, and motivational videos on YouTube (lol).

The majority of the world seems to follow this simple equation:

Academic excellence = financial and material abundance = "success" = happy humans!

However, this often equals "Spiritually malnourished humans, void of emotion and warmth".

Think of the difference between someone living in the city and someone living in the countryside.

Time moves faster in the city, it's expensive, the pressures to succeed are far heavier, influence is aggressive, knowledge is endless, efficiency is key, and rest is rescheduled.

Outside of the cities, it's almost the opposite. It's easier to move slowly and be present. Things are done properly and the people are down to earth. Everything's cheaper, health is wealth, stress is dormant, love is your currency, and balance is key.

The city demands you to grow up fast and to keep up. The country accepts you as you are.

The city never sleeps. The country sleeps in.

If you move to the city before you're fully grown, when will you take the time to finish growing?

KIDS RAISING KIDS

Some kids think that having kids of their own will help them grow up.

Some think having a business with employees makes them grow up.

Some compensate by doing grown-up things to mask their incompetence.

You can see how this leads to poor upbringings, right?

As a child, I also believed that "grownups" were no longer kids simply because they had kids, jobs, and mortgages, etc. I believed they had all the answers to everything. Naturally, I trusted them wholeheartedly.

I discovered that most "grownups" still have a lot of growing to do. (Apparently, there's no official age when you get your "adult" badge either? What a circus!)

Luckily, for us all, we're not obligated to do better, but you can clearly see when a person of authority is underqualified for their position.

I believe the issue here is that most students don't recognise this, and even if they did, there's not much they can do about it if they need their education.

> **Remember:** confidence and charisma can fool anyone into believing whatever you want.

My suggestion is not to send everyone to a therapist (even though that would be great), but to simply create better standards so we can all hold each other accountable.

THE IDEAL APPRENTICESHIP?

I doubt there will ever be a recipe for a "perfect apprenticeship", but how about we aim for something "a little less shit"?

Since it's mostly relative to the tattoo studio and the students themselves, it's very difficult to create a syllabus. This is why I'm suggesting something more natural.

It requires a bit more groundwork, compassion, and some mutual respect, but I think we can manage.

In a typical tattoo studio environment, communication is terrible, organisation is poor, respect is mostly absent, boundaries are nonexistent, and everyone is sleep deprived, and/or physically, emotionally, and spiritually malnourished.

Not a great recipe for a tasty dish, is it?

Now, bear with me here, this concept is a little far-out and likely the reason it's never been welcomed with open arms.

BEFORE HIRING AN APPRENTICE:

1. The environment must be functional and healthy through honest work. Compassionate communication should be mandatory. A healthy environment means no internal bias, no bitching, no unresolved conflicts, and no secrets.
2. High standards must be expected from all artists, managers, and new hires, with regular check-ins to maintain harmony. Leave no space for bad habits, poor values, and laziness. Hygiene must remain excellent at all times.
3. Company finances must be green. A financial incentive cannot be the main reason to hire an apprentice. No exceptions.
4. Everyone in the studio must be genuinely prepared for the extra workload, as having a new person around can be taxing. Make sure everyone understands and respects each other's responsibilities.
5. The primary teacher for an apprentice must be completely qualified. They must have enough proven skill and methods to provide a thorough education by themselves. Clear boundaries must be set if the other artists have different styles/methods. They must communicate if they feel others don't respect boundaries or disturb the process.
6. The primary teacher must have a syllabus or a clear structure of the education timeline (a draft will do) in order to hold themselves accountable. The apprentice should also receive a copy so they know what to expect. Be realistic, not ambitious.
7. The studio must establish realistic entry standards for an apprentice. An apprentice must be a good fit upon arrival, not just someone with potential. If they don't fit, don't make them fit, simply recommend somewhere else. No exceptions.

8. A one-month trial period must take place for all new apprentices, even if someone feels like a perfect fit. People must be tested for their true colours to show. Everyone deserves time to form their own opinion about what they're getting into.
9. Transparency is essential. An apprentice is a human above all else, and they're entitled to the truth. Hiring them is an equal exchange, one that all can be grateful for. No bullshit contracts.

UPON HIRING AN APPRENTICE:

1. Treat the one-month trial period the same as any other month of the year. Review and address everything before moving forward. Make sure everyone is heard and understood.
2. Make it very clear what's expected of the apprentice, and make sure they know what they can expect from their teacher. Again, be realistic, not ambitious.
3. Talk about money as soon as possible. It's the elephant in the room, and it will follow you everywhere. Come to a long-term agreement that's fair for all. Throwing a bunch of numbers around to sound clever will only emphasise one's incompetence.
4. Pace yourselves and stick to the plan. Rushing things is a sign of desperation that will only tarnish the chemistry between all involved.
5. Follow through. Don't start strong and let it fizzle out. Monitor progress and check in regularly to ensure the teacher and the apprentice remain energised.
6. Remain open-minded. It's likely an apprentice will offer new perspectives on the craft and be shut down immedi-

ately by a teacher. If it genuinely doesn't work, don't just tell them, show them why. If no one knows, say nothing until it's been tried and tested.
7. Don't support or spread information that only sounds right. The internet only shows the tip of the iceberg, and most people are full of shit. The vast majority of techniques and strategies are completely relative and subjective only to the artist sharing them.
8. Don't just regurgitate information from others unless you clearly apply it yourself. The apprentice has come to you for their apprenticeship. You are responsible—no one else. Make sure all artists are aware of external influence; it can spread quickly. (Example: if your apprentice sees a video of someone popular wearing a Rolex whilst they're tattooing and then begins wearing a watch whilst they're tattooing as well, this is on YOU, not them. YOU are responsible for educating your apprentice and they should know better, way before they start tattooing.)
9. Don't make the apprentice settle for anything less than your best effort. If an apprentice has a valid question and you don't have the answer, then you must find the answer together. Don't tell them to ask someone else; this only suggests you're incompetent.
10. Don't hesitate to do what's necessary. If someone turns sour or if something is out of your control, you must ultimately do what's best for you and your studio. Act rationally, exchange gratitude, and come to the best possible agreement before you part ways. Bad blood will fester among the community if it isn't taken care of. Act responsibly.

Regardless of what I believe could work, it all boils down to our collective efforts to support a healthier environment overall.

As an individual, you have far more power than you realise to preserve the purity of your creative heart. The more you reaffirm your own values, the more you will become immune to negative forces.

Look out for *you*.

Topic #5

Stay True to YOU

You know those days when everything's a struggle? You're trying real hard but your head's up your ass, and you've misplaced your pencil seven times already.

Imagine you feel like that almost every day, and you can't seem to catch a break. That's what it feels like to be unaligned, just a touch less complicated.

It's like trying to pull out in third gear, failing to understand why you keep stalling, and still blaming the car for your misery.

Or stubbornly looking for your glasses in the dark because you're too lazy to turn the light on, and blaming your parents for giving birth to you in the first place.

Things don't make sense when you're misaligned, and that much becomes very clear once you decide to look in the mirror.

The day I finally quit working for my previous studio, I realised I'd never felt completely aligned with myself and that the real hard work was just beginning.

To be *aligned* with yourself is to feel like you're living true to your own human nature and your own interests. You feel at peace more often than not, and it's very rare you have nasty, anxious feelings ruling your gut.

When we're *out* of alignment, we tend to chase our own tails and suffer as a result. We favour a victim mentality, and despite our best efforts, we continue to struggle until we fully *commit* to the detox we need.

And by detox, I simply mean distancing yourself from external ideologies, expectations, and social obligations for a strict period of time in order to regain a sense of stillness in your mind.

THE TATTER TOT

There once was a tatter tot (apprentice tattoo artist) who risked it all for a dream. He wasn't the most confident lad, but he was ready to do whatever it took. He met a bunch of mysterious tatters, all shapes and sizes. He took advice from all because "they knew best".

Months later, he was doing whatever dirty work they asked him to. They constantly made fun of the clothes he loved to wear—bullied him like schoolkids, just for a laugh. He figured they wouldn't make fun of him if he just dressed more like them, right?

And so it began.

Social media made it easier to see how cool everyone else looked. So, why not explore how he could make himself cooler? Face tattoos are trending. Fuck it. Vapes? He got two. Anything to blend in so he could focus on being a team player.

Months passed, and he was still met with resistance. His best was never good enough.

These guys loved harassing our dear tatter tot. Shit, they were convinced it would actually make him a tougher person *and* a better tattoo artist. "Our apprenticeship was super tough. We had to eat shit every day, and we didn't even get paid! So, consider yourself lucky."

Tatter took it all onboard, and now that his first year had passed, it was time for a trip back to the shire. His parents barely recognised him. They missed his handsome face and the lovely shirts he used to wear. "This is who I am now. You guys should get used to it."

Poor Tatter had joined the dark side.

Now that he'd fully committed, he must've believed it himself, right?

See, this is where it gets interesting.

Since the beginning, he'd never actually checked in with himself. He'd been avoiding those mirrors for a while too. He was never seen without his earphones—he loved blocking out the noise with more noise. Anytime his thoughts came creeping in, he'd find a way to silence them.

Can you blame him? It made the grind much easier.

His boss needed someone to tattoo his associates who worked on the shop. Tatter volunteered, working himself to the bone, in hopes for a little respect.

What he didn't realise was that he'd just made himself the yes-man for favours. And with poor Tatter having no boundaries, the bossman took him for a ride.

This went on for a disturbingly long time until the headaches turned to migraines, and the migraines turned to breakdowns. He'd been cancelling and moving so many of his appointments that his clients went somewhere else.

His body was telling him something, and this time, he had no choice but to listen.

He laid down his pride for a moment and surrendered.

All he wanted was to learn how to tattoo and make art for people.

How on earth did this happen?

TAKE A STEP BACK

It's easy to get led astray or pulled away from yourself at times, especially in this industry. It'll likely happen for a long time, too, at least until you begin to resonate with who you are.

I grew up thinking I had to discover myself through trying lots of new things. I was constantly seeking things that felt right—those "things" being my clothes, my friends, my art style, my habits, etc.

Everything felt right…until it didn't, and I was back on the hunt.

Not once did I ever stop to actually ask myself questions in solitude. And even if I did, it's unlikely I would've valued the answers anyway.

I'm bringing awareness to these topics in hopes that *you* will gain a little extra time, feeling at home in your *own* mind and body.

It seems naive to even suggest that I could help you avoid turbulence. But to at least hold you *still*—just for a moment—and invite you to look within, that would be pretty cool.

OPEN YOUR HEART

We all want to be loved in the eyes of everyone else, but what about the eyes of ourselves?

We grind tirelessly, day and night, to acquire things and create this idea of ourselves. This includes working really hard at what we do in order to be admired and respected by others—simply for doing what we do.

The thing that was once our hobby has been put on steroids and now controls our self-worth. (Sounds like most tattoo shop owners, doesn't it?)

When you started tattooing, were you prepared for how much it was going to drag you all over the place?

When social media became a tool for promotion, did you expect it to hijack your identity and make you doubt every single thing you worked hard for?

Well, that shit *happened* and it's still *happening*.

In our most impressionable years, being surrounded by our peers and role models (most of whom have strong, influential personalities too), we don't realise that we're a part of this giant invisible shitstorm.

"I heard so and so uses this machine." Without a second thought, we drop the machine we've only been using for two weeks. Never even gave it a chance.

"Wow, this person made a reel of them doing dumb shit. It went viral, and now they have 100K followers." Without a second thought, we're doing the same dumb shit, praying it'll go viral.

What's more insane is that this type of behaviour is actually supported and, in some cases, *encouraged*.

I get it. Any publicity is good publicity and all that jazz. But where is our integrity, and why are we so desperate?

No wonder we get so confused and upset when our best approach to life is to copy everyone else and always be late to the party.

I mean, it was never supposed to be this way, right? In theory, working with a bunch of cool dudes, making tats and smoking weed every day is the dream, right? How could that become dysfunctional?

Breathe...it's not that deep.

Topic #6

Beware of the Vampires

In this topic, I will be opening the curtains and letting the sunshine pour in. It's time to expose a certain breed of parasite in our industry and expedite the extinction process. (It's a metaphor. Relax.)

Without further ado, please welcome the energy vampires!

I like to visualise this topic as a big bundle of garlic. Kinda weird, sure.

However, vampires *hate* garlic, just like the energy vampires in our industry are gonna *hate* this topic.

By definition, energy vampires are people who prey on the good will of others and drain them of all their positive energy. This is highly common in a workplace environment, especially when positive energy and knowledge can be scarce.

Although some energy vampires are oblivious to their injustices, they can be just as draining (and often more so) as those who know they are a drain.

At first, we have no idea what's happening to us since

the effects aren't always instantaneous. In some cases, the damage grows over time, and we suspect it's our own doing. (Sneaky little shits, aren't they?)

Quick questions, though: Do you ambush people in search of knowledge? Do you ask people for things before you even consider how they're doing? Do you desperately compensate with your weak sense of humour because your tattoos are also weak?

If the answer is yes, it sounds like you could be down with the sickness. Fear not, my child. You're safe now.

Let's begin by identifying the various types of energy vampires that lurk in our realm.

CHOOSE YOUR VAMPIRE

1. **The Manipulator:** This person will masterfully convince you to do what they want you to do whilst simultaneously convincing you that this is what you wanted to do the entire time. Manipulators are the best at using persuasion tactics and gaslighting to get what they want, often leaving their victims confused and exhausted.
2. **The Minimizer:** We all know someone who loves to put others down in order to build themselves up. Regardless of your best efforts, a minimizer will find any reason to dwarf your achievements, leaving you feeling small in comparison.
3. **The Dependent:** This poor soul is fuelled by support and reassurance from others. They often lack any sense of initiative, struggling to make the simplest decisions for themselves. They drain others with their constant need for guidance and advice.
4. **The Controller:** A controller thinks they have all the answers. They insist on telling everyone what to do and will often hijack a situation, demanding authority.
5. **The Victim:** Victim vampires are known for exaggerating anything that may happen to them. Using any bait they can, they spend their time fishing for sympathy, reeling in anyone they can. VVs are exhausting to be around not only because they demand your attention, but their negative perception of life will feel like a dark rain cloud, following you around.
6. **The Narcissist:** According to these vampires, they're the most important in the room. Two in the same room is unimaginable. These attention-seeking, tenacious, insatiable little parasites will work tirelessly to suck you dry.
7. **The Curveball Vampire:** This funky beast is your worst nightmare. They're like the illegitimate love child of all the

other vampires. You never know what you're gonna get with these guys. They'll keep you guessing, holding you hostage on the emotional roller coaster that they operate.

> Before we start pointing fingers, it's time to look in that mirror. (Do it.)
>
> Personally, I've done my fair share of sucking the life out of people. I knew I was a burden to the homies. I just couldn't see a way out.
>
> It's important to address this topic with a heart full of empathy and compassion. Especially with yourself. If you're found guilty of such crimes, please be gentle with yourself and proceed with caution.

Vampires in our industry don't mean to be draining; they're just a little lost.

Some of the sweetest people I know have been energy vampires and they weren't even aware of it. If they were, they certainly wouldn't be proud of the adverse effects they've had on people.

Nonetheless, they must be dealt with (humanely).

Our tattoo studios and creative spaces are sacred to us; we work tirelessly to keep them nice and clean. We even pay the tax man half every month, simply to continue existing.

So I ask you this: why do the vampires get to live rent-free, like black mould in our walls?

Sure, you can run, block, and ostracise the vampires all you like. Save yourself. But if you're not the victim, then someone else will be.

You'll feel better for a while, but the bloodsuckers continue walking the halls, draining your precious team, one by one.

Your people need you. Hell, even the vampires need you.

I'm not saying pierce silver stakes through their chests, but at least give them hugs and open some tough conversations. Show some team spirit and give a shit in a useful way.

We all know how a bad apple ruins the whole fruit bowl, and this is especially true in a tattoo shop. Anyone with six months of experience knows this.

What good is bitching about our vampires and turning our backs on them? If we can do that to a member of our team, then what does that say about us?

It's true, some people just aren't a good match. But trying to master synergy in large groups of young adults requires a team effort.

The modern world has made it so easy for us to dissociate, not just with our noise-cancelling headphones, but by creating this appeal for us to grind and heartlessly push and shove our way through the crowd.

Instead of being attentive and gentle with our neighbours, we're advised to look out for ourselves by any means necessary.

Sure, you've gotta focus on yourself, and technically the vampires should help themselves too. But are you willing to return once you're energised in case the vampires still need you?

I'm merely putting emphasis on the people in your circles here. Your best friends, your brothers and sisters, your colleagues, and especially the new apprentice. They all deserve more than your cold shoulder.

HOW TO DEAL WITH ENERGY VAMPIRES

1. **Don't internalise their criticisms:** Don't measure yourself against the standards set for you by an energy vampire. Remind yourself that criticism from others tells you more about them than it does about yourself. I'm not suggesting you identify as better than them. Just don't give them that power over you.
2. **Set clear boundaries:** Healthy boundaries are essential to ensuring stable relationships. When you set a boundary, you are creating limits on what others can ask of you and what you're willing to give.
3. **Don't expect them to be something they are not:** The only person we can change is ourself. Try to lead by example. Become that person you want to be around. Don't waste time trying to force the energy vampire to change. Instead, spend time taking care of your own needs.
4. **Prioritise self-care:** Energy vampires will drain you any chance they can. Prioritising self-care is essential to remaining aligned. Take time to meditate and do whatever gives you energy. Regularly checking in with yourself and strengthening your awareness will make this easier over time.
5. **Be up-front and direct:** When someone is taking advantage of your kindness, it is important to be assertive and call out the bad behaviour. This doesn't mean pull them aside and ruin their day. Just get your foot in the door and communicate. The longer you allow the draining behaviour to continue, the harder it will be to stop.
6. **Don't feed them by overreacting:** Energy vampires feed on the chaos and drama they create. By refusing to give them what they want, you are shutting down the cycle that leaves you drained and keeps them charged up. Remain

calm and spread awareness of this behaviour. They won't last long.
7. **Don't feel guilty for taking space:** Guilting people is one way that energy vampires fulfil their needs. Don't let anyone make you feel guilty for taking control of your own life. Vampires aren't completely hopeless. In most cases, distancing yourself can be the wake-up call a vampire needs.

So, I'm sure you're thinking that's fairly contradictory in contrast to how I rambled on before (and if so, I'd say how dare you!).

However, you're not completely wrong.

Doing what's best for you doesn't automatically give you a free pass to be an asshole and turn your back on a vampire.

Just imagine the big picture for a sec: as a victim, you're incapable of making a change. First, you must level up.

If possible, take some space, set those boundaries, rest up, and return to the battlefield stronger than ever.

We do not turn our backs on our own. This is partly why tattoo artists are constantly on rotation, jumping from shop to shop, never seeming to find peace.

It's partly why your boss is quick to throw someone out and hire the next kid with a dream. It's much easier to shuffle your cards and hope for a better one instead of working with what you've got.

Am I spiralling? Is this a byproduct of our throw-away culture? Possibly.

Let's get back on track.

How do you know if you're in a supportive environment?

Most people would assume that we're all in supportive environments. Sadly, this is not the case.

Most artists claim to be met with resistance whenever they attempt to be more positive.

Remember, it's a lot easier to just put your headphones on and drown out the noise for another day than it is to open a difficult conversation at the studio.

Try these three things:

1. Assess whether or not your peers encourage/support you to do something difficult. Do they simply suggest the easy road?
2. Pay attention to the gaslighting. Do people suggest you're being dramatic when you have an issue with them or others?
3. Get some perspective. Distance yourself from the studio, ideally for longer than a weekend, and really think about the team dynamic. Write down your thoughts instead of juggling them in your head.

Of course, it's not that simple. It's quite difficult to detect the roots of the dysfunction. This is exactly why I encourage you to take it seriously before you try to heroically jump in and save the world or start pointing fingers.

Remember: most of your colleagues are busy with their own projects and desires every day. Attempting to improve the health of the team is not their priority, nor will it be a popular idea, hence why I'm encouraging you to do it anyway.

"Your inward conflicts express themselves in outward disasters."
—kriShnaMurti

Topic #7

A Little Validation

So let's dive into something a little less intense and start clearing this mess up.

The industry isn't all bad. In fact, it's far from it.

There's something so very special about it that tells me I'll be making tattoos until my hands no longer work—unless I get a sweet bionic arm upgrade in the future (come on, scientists).

In that case, I'll be making tattoos for people until the very day I transcend. Then, I will be reincarnated as a golden retriever and, therefore, unable to make tattoos as we know them.

Thus, if this is my only chance to leave a mark on the industry, you must understand why I have no choice.

I refuse to play dead if there's still a chance that another human could find peace because of my efforts.

I never knew how aggressive the desire for validation was until I entered the art world.

Regardless of where it comes from, we cannot deny the hunger for it until we become our very own source. And to achieve such a gift is a long and tedious pilgrimage.

In my experience, some people have been lucky to enter the industry without a need for external validation ("lucky" in a sense that they were unshakeable). Yet such luck only hindered their growth as an artist, leaving them with a deep sense of isolation because they were unable to utilise criticism.

On the other hand, others are born into the industry like a newborn calf. Regardless of age and experience in other fields, the tattoo industry will catch them off guard and strip them bare.

These people unknowingly give all their power to everyone but themselves every time they express doubt or show weakness.

Naturally, this, too, will hinder growth, leaving you spread all over the place. You'll be constantly built up and broken down every time you create and release.

Your codependency on the opinions of others will teach you that your self-worth is in their hands, causing a constant sense of emptiness when you're alone.

No human should yearn for the praise of others, for they are the ultimate source already.

I suggest you aim for a reasonable space between both of these extremities.

If we were taught to love and support ourselves the same way we offer it to others, we'd have a far richer source to offer it from. Not only would we grow into stronger beings, capable and dependant by ourselves, but we would be valuable assets to all around us.

External validation should not be a currency that helps us indicate our self-worth. It most certainly shouldn't be a rating system for our artistic abilities.

REALITY

It's likely you entered the industry hoping everyone would be nice and supportive.

It's highly likely that you grew up thinking the world would be that way too.

What a shitty surprise that was, huh?

The world consists of a lot of hurt people who haven't realised they're hurt and people who know they're hurting and are relentlessly projecting it outward.

These are the people who may challenge you the most, and as an empathetic, sensitive artist, you'll likely attract them like a moth to a flame.

This is why I recommend a little training.

Here's how you can begin to be your own source of validation:

1. **Recognise Your Achievements:** Don't mistake this for being full of yourself. Simply take a moment to acknowledge and celebrate your achievements, big or small. Be proud of yourself for your efforts. Whether it's completing a piece of art, overcoming a personal challenge, or simply preparing a nice meal, give yourself credit. You must do this in solitude; otherwise, it defeats the purpose.
2. **Set Realistic Goals:** Set easily achievable goals for yourself. The first step here is to establish your current capabilities. When you reach a goal, it reinforces a sense of accomplishment and self-worth. The more you consistently achieve your goals, you will become reliable for yourself and watch yourself become the version you dreamed of. Note: don't be too hard on yourself if things don't go as planned; this is what stops most people. You must be gentle and stay on track.

3. **Trust Your Instincts:** As an artist, your intuition is a powerful guide. Trust your creative instincts and recognise that your unique perspective is valuable. Your work doesn't have to conform to anyone else's standards—especially if the person is not creative themselves. Naturally this will be tough if there's no market for your style, but you either swallow your desires or follow the market. Either way, you must commit.
4. **Learn from Mistakes:** Mistakes are a natural part of the creative process. Do you expect a newborn child to be able to run a marathon at all, let alone be the best at it? If you're not so good at something then you're likely new to it (and if you're not new, then it's probably not for you). However, instead of seeing mistakes as failures, view them as an attempt that wasn't quite there yet. You only fail when you give up. Embrace the journey. Without bad stuff, good stuff would just be stuff, and nothing would mean anything.
5. **Surround Yourself with Positivity:** Seek out supportive and constructive feedback from those who genuinely appreciate your work. If you're currently surrounded by superficial assholes who just tell you what you want to hear, pack your bags. Surrounding yourself with positivity can help reinforce your belief in your abilities. Remember, positive people don't wanna be around you if you're not genuinely positive. If you're still a dependent energy vampire, then you'll only make life difficult for everyone involved. Learn and proceed when the time is right.
6. **Reflect on Your Progress:** Regularly reflect on your artistic journey and personal growth. Seeing how far you've come can be a powerful reminder of your capabilities. If you're not happy with your progress, then I suggest you

dig a little deeper. We often get stuck and don't know how to improve our situations; this is where a professional can help you enormously.

7. **Cultivate Self-Compassion:** Treat yourself with the same kindness and understanding that you would offer a friend facing challenges. Imagine that adorable child version of you; how would you support them? Self-compassion goes a long way towards building a healthy support system. It'll act as your trusty compass in a multitude of scenarios. (Bonus, this will naturally strengthen your compassion for others.)

Being your own source of validation is an ongoing process, and you will likely be met with resistance. Negative people feel uncomfortable around positive people who wish to improve themselves. Please, do not be discouraged.

Do better for you so you can do better for others.

Topic #8

The Craft

The idea of being a tattoo artist seems so confusing when you're in it.

When it started gaining popularity in the Western tradition, it was as simple as making some sweet drawings and tattooing them on people in exchange for a pack of smokes or some pennies.

Naturally, we've evolved, and today we have so many options for every single aspect of tattooing:

- Which machine will I use?
- Which needles?
- Who do I wanna get sponsored by?
- Which ink is the best?
- Why is everything so fucking expensive?
- Will face tats ruin my life?
- Which style should I make?
- Which studios should I work in?
- Which cities charge the most money for tattoos?
- Who gives the best advice?

- How do I make my designs more original?
- How do I get more Instagram followers?
- Do I need to make TikToks as well?
- Can I make a living from it, and how soon?

So many decisions.

Just because we *can* do all these things, and we *can* consider all the options, we *must*, right? Wrong.

This is why, I believe, it begins to get confusing and difficult for a lot of people.

Not a lot of people will settle for average when they know it's possible to achieve greatness. Especially if they've felt neglected or inferior their whole life and believe that tattooing is their one shot at salvation.

It's not tattooing that's confusing—it's the people making the tattoos.

SQUARES IN CIRCULAR PLACES

In this scenario, I like to think of a "sorting cube" (the popular puzzle for children).

We have cylinders, cubes, hexagons, triangles, stars, and various other shapes, all with a desire to enter the cube. However, each shape can only enter the cube through its very own door, designed specifically for it.

Sure, you can try to force them through other doors—and sometimes you'll be successful—but the square may become a circle in the process.

The tattoo industry (and the world) has a lot of differently shaped people trying to squeeze themselves through any door they can without realising what shape they are first, and completely oblivious to the fact that there are even doors. All to reside within a cube (the industry) with any level of ability, simply to sustain a living.

DO LESS

There is a Taoist principle known as "wu-wei," meaning to take action in a natural or effortless way. It directly translates to *nonaction*, commonly known as nondoing.

A wu-wei mindset implies that trying less can generate more. To surrender and relax facilitates a sense of effortless and more flow state experiences, which opens the door to peak performance.

In our world, this can be understood as knowing when to take a break because your design looks shit and you're seconds away from putting your head in the microwave.

Wu-wei suggests that if you must force yourself through a door, it's unlikely you were meant to be there in the first place.

Instead of forcing it and blaming the locks, you must surrender to the resistance, smile, and try another door.

In other words, it helps to have a clue about how you operate naturally as a person before approaching a new doorway. It may save you a great deal of time and energy, and you certainly won't feel like a Jehovah's Witness.

It may seem unnecessary at first, but having a better understanding of what we actually do for a living can make things a hell of a lot easier.

It can also help us identify whether we're moving towards our ideal life, running from our past, or simply spinning around in funny little circles.

WE CAN'T ALL BE LEAD SINGERS

Think of it like members of a traditional rock band. They're all equally important, yet for whatever reason, one becomes the lead singer, another the lead guitarist, the drummer, and so on.

They each commit to all responsibilities and pressures to remain in their position. They always have a choice to be there, and they understand what's expected of them. They simply wouldn't be on stage if it wasn't for everyone playing their part.

Imagine they all wanted to play the drums. Not gonna work, is it?

Each member of the band gravitates towards their specialty because they love it more than any other option, and they own it and stay in their lane so that the entire band can harmonise.

They didn't just decide to start a band with no musical experience and then guess which instrument to play for five years before they started playing seriously. That would be a recipe for disaster.

The Singer: All the style, their very own brand

- Must create a legacy
- Big dreams
- Will stop at nothing for success

Loves: Attention, praise, respect, the craft, the fans, the sponsors, the idea of themselves, the sound of their own voice, living rent-free in the heads of their haters

Hates: Themselves, setting up/cleaning their own work station, emails, haters, criticism, making stencils, "the algorithm", being called a diva

The Guitarist: Humble, nerdy, loves the craft

- Just wants to do what they love
- Cares about the industry
- People pleaser

Loves: Getting technical, the flow, the companionship, new toys and gadgets, their dog, their loyal clientele, progress

Hates: Being interrupted, greed, drama, repetition, sleeping, salespeople

The Bassist: Maintains rhythm, loves the balance

- Can't imagine doing anything else
- Equilibrium is the goal
- Keeps it simple

Loves: Family, longevity, harmony in all moments, doing their part, eating, contributing

Hates: Cold coffee, working on weekends, spontaneous events, cancellations, sassiness

The Drummer: High energy, ready for whatever

- Ride or die for the craft
- Old-school mentality
- Loud

Loves: The craft, farting in public, dumb shit, energy drinks, making people laugh, anarchy

Hates: Silence, clients who move or complain, pandemics, the tax man

The Manager: The business type, doesn't care much for the craft

- Follows the money
- Always reading books about the grind
- Ambassador for materialism

Loves: Entrepreneurs, people they can gain from, following trends, "stimulants", posting pics of their shopping sprees, the idea of being famous

Hates: NCAs, FOMO, sleeping, emotions, people not hustling 24/7, traffic, and pedestrians

The Groupie: The good-looking one, just wants to be a part of the group

- Started making tattoos because "the aesthetic is cute"
- Has no idea what an autoclave is
- Overcompensates with their physical attributes

Loves: Vacation, attention, being hot, a daily OOTD post, getting paid, TikTok trends, tips/gifts from clients, stealing flash

Hates: Long sessions, waiting, criticism, being alone, hard work, cleaning the shop, not being taken seriously

You may know someone like this, or you may be someone like this yourself. We all tend to adopt a persona to survive in a tattoo shop, and in life in general.

We often drop the mask when no one's watching; becoming aware of this can definitely work in your favour.

It's not a crisis unless you're in denial; I prefer to think of it as a gift.

> Naturally, this part may upset a lot of you because it will reflect upon your insecurities. I'm not sorry for hurting your feelings. I'm just sorry you've been misled and feel out of place. I'm sorry you feel like you have to compensate or act differently because you were led to believe you're not good enough as you are.

AT WHAT COST?

The reason I'm writing this part is because a lot of people are forcing themselves to love something they don't truly love, and it's hurting the entire ecosystem. Some of you know you're in the wrong place. Some of you don't realise it yet, and some of you will refuse to admit it. A fraction of you will even push through and succeed, but at what cost?

The world doesn't need more tattoo artists, just like we don't need more influencers or YouTubers wasting our time and energy. We just need the current ones to do better.

Becoming a tattoo artist shouldn't be something you just stumble upon because you're running out of ideas for a career.

The craft was once sacred because of its scarcity of skilled and dedicated artists. Now it's overpopulated because we're promoting this idea that people can do whatever they want and that anyone can become a tattoo artist if they want to.

First of all, most of us don't even know what we truly want at any given moment in time. If we already knew, we wouldn't have to think about it so much.

Sure, you *could* become a tattoo artist, but maybe don't unless there's a restless force inside you dying to be unleashed. Unless you solemnly swear to be an honest practitioner and representative of this industry. Unless you're willing and committed to doing everything it requires without complaining and praying for easy solutions. Unless you're in love with almost every moment you operate as a tattoo artist, the pressure, the cleaning, the drawing, the stencils, the complicated chats with clients and your boss, the sleepless nights and anxiety, and the financial stresses.

Unless you're confident it's for you, please don't force it to be.

By all means give it a shot, but if every sign in the world is telling you otherwise, then listen.

A RECIPE FOR INSANITY

For the people currently considering if this is the life for them, please close your eyes and imagine this scenario.

> Audiobook listeners, please actually close your eyes. Readers, do not.

Picture this: It's 3:00 p.m. on a sunny Friday. It's busier than ever in the tattoo shop, the radio's on repeat, and you left your headphones at home, people are being people, you're running on coffee and cigs, so you're feeling splendid; someone left their screaming, snotty baby on the couch, the shop phone is ringing, and the manager already went home; now your client's girlfriend is repeatedly sighing because she's bored. On top of that, your client won a giveaway and asked you to rework their twenty-year-old tribal all day, so you're getting paid in high-fives.

How is your state of mind right now?

Do you still love this life?

Can you survive a year?

Will you happily tolerate the aches and pains from sitting on your ass for a living?

Do creative ideas pour out of you endlessly, regardless of your peers?

Do you believe your art could bring joy to other people?

Could you be an asset to all around you as a tattoo artist?

Or was becoming a tattoo artist simply a last resort?

Are you easily influenced by others into making big decisions?

Are you in too deep?

Do you simply love the idea of it all?

Does it seem like a safer option than pursuing your true passion or life's purpose?

These questions should help you identify whether or not you are suited for the craft.

The desire to draw something and eternalise it on someone is a beautifully weird fetish to have, and truly loving it should come naturally.

If you're only at peace in this career on the good days, then you'll likely be miserable for a long, long time.

Topic #9

The Pursuit of Originality

I've always had this omnipresent hunger for originality. I felt I'd tried everything, gravitating towards anything new or different, relying solely on validation from the outside world, only to discover that I was missing the point entirely. Originality within the tattoo industry is not a destination, but a pursuit.

You can acknowledge something you like when you see it, but don't get off your own bus to try and grab it, because you'll only be left with a lot of catching up to do.

Think of it as a dance. Do you dare to perform moves that no one's seen before? Even at the risk of rejection or embarrassment? Even if you do it in private and it feels incredible?

Let's say you do the funky chicken for the first time. The room goes silent. You have two choices:

1. You can pretend it was a joke, and go back to playing it safe.
2. You can own it and mind your business.

All it takes is for one other person to reciprocate that energy—before you know it, the entire room is bouncing around like chickens.

The goal is not to get people to copy you or to copy others, but to grow accustomed to expressing yourself without hesitation. So that when a new idea or desire comes to mind you don't even stop for a moment to consider a horrible outcome.

If we constantly live in our comfort zone, only exploring what we know, we avoid any responsibility to contribute relative to our capabilities. Not only that, but we obstruct the flow of energy that the world *requires* to avoid stagnancy and regression.

I know it's tough. We get stuck in this loop of making the same things over and over until our precious heads explode. Yet we put on a smile and get it done because it pays the bills, right? One moment we're okay; the next we're crying in the prep room wondering what the *fuck* just happened.

We have too much to lose, so we're overleveraged and don't have a choice, right?

This is true to an extent. A lot of us feel paralysed because we have children, dogs, houses, and other commitments. Therefore, tattooing has become a chore since it's our main source of income.

The owner of the tattoo shop loves to dangle that carrot every time we imply we're not happy. "You just need to chill a little more, post more on Instagram. One day you'll have a shop of your own and be able to tattoo whatever you want, charge whatever you want, and take as many days off as you want."

And so the cycle continues.

Sure, sometimes strength prevails, and we try to break through; yet, sometimes we post that design, and it doesn't sell, so our brains assume we suck. No wonder we go back to our shells and stay there. It can be rough outside.

However, imagine this: One day you remove expectations and ideas. On *this* day you truly love that design and you *mean* it. You release it into the world, but you don't sit around waiting. You let it go and know you're worthy. The next morning, a client DMs you saying, "How soon can we make this?" Jackpot! You nail that tattoo. You honour your achievement and share it with your audience. Another client witnesses your greatness, and now the ball is rolling.

The important part is, do you believe you're worthy of this reality?

I know it sounds simple in theory, and we all know it's not. So now I ask you this: do you truly love what you make? I'm talking about the ideas and designs and projects you dream of creating, even if in secret. Does your audience and clientele *believe* you genuinely love your own art? Why would they even want it on their bodies if there's no soul to it, right?

ASK YOURSELF BETTER QUESTIONS

An important part of our journey as artists is discovering those really juicy questions that leave us puzzled.

We tend to think it's about how well we can answer questions/resolve issues, yet this becomes quickly ineffective when our questions barely scratch the surface.

If you're not happy with where you are, what makes you think you're single-handedly capable of evolving?

Are you dissatisfied with your work? Is your imposter syndrome simply true because you don't *actually* know what you're doing? Perhaps you're on the wrong path entirely. Do you find yourself following trends and making tattoos that everyone else is making? Are you sad you're always "too tired" to make designs for yourself because you're so busy? When exactly do you plan to not be tired? You know it takes longer than a weekend to recover, so when will you hack back your time and energy?

First, take a deep breath. Whoever told you this was an easy career was a good ol' fashioned liar.

The good news is, you're here now. You're doing something good for yourself. Reading this book is your way of saying, "I am aware of these things and I will do better".

> It might seem like I'm making everything deep and confusing, but for real, the industry needs *you* to give a shit (even more than you currently do).

My theory here is that the pursuit of originality begins when you no longer allow your fear of failure to govern your mind:

- You let go of your attachment and sense of control.
- You create with no expectations of a reward.
- You begin to support yourself and take chances for a brighter future.
- You encourage others to take chances, too, and in time, they're able to reciprocate that energy.
- You hold each other up, and your team becomes a healthy, reliable, and charismatic system.
- You fight for quality over quantity and promote rest and nourishment. You push back when you're met with resistance, and you do it with integrity.

- You establish standards and boundaries and actually respect them.

In other words, the internet doesn't have the answer. It has inspiration and references for your *ideas*.

The journey begins at your own front door, and you're the only one with the key.

Topic #10

Practice and Patience

As a teenager, I knew how much I loved the process. I loved drawing and creating something from nothing. The thought of mastery didn't even cross my mind until further down the line. I never let the pressure obstruct my joy because I had no worries of what the future held. I didn't have taxes or bills or major expenses to worry about. What a life, huh?

I'm aware it was a huge privilege. I know I was lucky I had the space and support to nurture my passion as a teen. Especially in the world today. I was one of the few born in the right place at the right time.

But as social media made it increasingly easier to communicate with the world, I slowly began to trade my current joy for the idea of more joy in the future.

Kinda like the party game: "Would you rather have €100 every day for the rest of your life, or €10,000,000 when you're sixty?"

Some don't care for true mastery of the craft. That much has become very clear to me. Some love the idea of identifying as "masters" for the benefits that follow. Some love the craft for all the wrong reasons. And luckily, some fall and remain in love, driven with that curiosity they possessed as children.

Tattooing is just another media for artists. No one is born to be a tattoo artist. You just naturally gravitate towards it because it's another avenue of expression for the fire within you.

If you lose that love or simply lack it to begin with, then you exist as an empty shell, operating under false pretences, doing whatever you can to replicate a sense of genuine passion, only to chase the dragon until you wake up or sleep forever.

This is why we constantly rely on our future selves to deliver us to a place of greatness. Or for the universe to bless us with life hacks and shortcuts that make our lives easier.

It's not that those of our latest generation don't want to do the hard work; they just simply do not love what they're working for.

It's just a paycheck, and to work smarter is to work less. They want to skip to the good parts and bathe in the glory.

STOP WISHING YOUR LIFE AWAY

One of the most heartbreaking and difficult things to deal with in our industry is our collective impatience.

I've met so many people in the past nine years who have suffered from their own impatience more than they've suffered from anything else.

There are multiple factors that contribute to a lack of patience when it comes to mastery of a skill. Here are a few important ones:

1. Lack of interest
2. Low value of current self
3. Financial pressure
4. Unrealistic expectations
5. Fear of failure and disappointment

I personally suffered from my impatience for a long time. Despite having a solid foundation of creative experience, I was never truly satisfied with the quality of my work or my current reality.

For the most part, I was encouraged to never be satisfied or celebrate my achievements.

To verbally praise your efforts can be confused with getting cocky, if falling on deaf ears.

I'd been tattooing for about six years when I first realised I'd misunderstood the entire art of reflection. My peers never exercised a healthy balance. It's one extreme or the other. Some can argue, "You'll never be satisfied". Some say, "When you're satisfied, you stop developing", or some classic nonsense like, "Stay hungry, bro".

They're not wrong. It's just such an easy response that it often tends to avoid reflection altogether.

Most advice we give and take is subconscious drivel that we learn from the interwebs and later regurgitate in the hope that we appear knowledgeable.

THE PURSUIT

To pursue ultimate mastery of the craft is romantic. It's admirable. It gives us a sense of accomplishment, and it's sexy in the eyes of all around us.

A modern-day disciplinarian—never satisfied, never proud, restless throughout their pursuit of perfection.

One can argue that we'll never quite get there. Personally, I love that. Like finally, truly, deep in my soul, I've found peace in surrendering to the idea that I'd rather not get there.

Think about it like a movie. It's the build up we all enjoy, the intense pursuit, the foreplay. The end is boring. Someone finally gets what they want, and the credits start rolling.

If you're constantly pushing the fast-forward button in hopes that you'll enjoy the ending, it implies the movie's complete shit, right?

News flash: *the movie* is your life, and you're the director. If it's shit, and you're hoping for the better parts instead of creating them, then you'll be pretty disappointed with the ending.

And worse, once the end credits start rolling in this life, you don't get to rewind and enjoy it all over again.

The thoughts start pouring in, along with all the berating of *shoulda done more* and *if only*.

Once this finally clicked for me, I had an epiphany.

It went something like this:

Damn, this movie is actually pretty special. I don't want to fast-forward to the end where I'm a sexy creative genius with a thick moustache, praised by all for my accomplishments and contributions to the industry. I want to make every scene last as long as possible, oozing with magic as though it were produced and directed by the most astonishing creator of all time. To fast-forward the process is to run faster to the grave. To wish I was better is to wish I wasn't here right now. I'm not wishing my life away, right? Maybe I am unhappy right now. Time to have a meeting with the director.

IT'S ALL BACKWARDS

Something that helped open my mind was a speech from my favourite speaker of all time, Alan Watts.

This gentleman promoted a healthy philosophy called "The Backwards Law".

It's the idea that the more you pursue something, the more you only confirm the fact that you lack it in the first place.

To constantly improve only reinforces your current weakness.

The more you seek beauty, the less beautiful you will be.

The longer you pursue mastery, the longer you must endure mediocrity.

We only know greatness in contrast to something less than greatness.

To define greatness is to compare it to something less than, whether it be your latest work or the work of your peers.

It's not to suggest that you shouldn't pursue anything at all, but avoid becoming a slave to the pursuit itself, and trust that you will improve naturally through time.

Embrace the present moment, and you will find peace in *all* that *is*.

Nurture a love for the process, and become one with the

good *and* the bad, the sun as well as the rain, for they are equals.

Flirt with the idea of mastery, but remain at a healthy distance before mastery gets creeped out.

The ultimate achievement is to open your mind to every second in the present moment, free of judgement.

Alan also compared the process to a dance routine, which is still, by far, my favourite way to relate to the creative process.

In simple terms, the purpose of the dance is not where the dancer ends up on the floor, nor is it how fast they get there.

The purpose of the dance *is* the dance itself.

It's the choreography, the charisma, the expression on the dancer's face, the commitment, and the flow that keeps you enchanted the entire time.

It's obvious when their heart's not in it. It's often unbearable and boring.

It's also very obvious when you watch someone make a tattoo when their heart's not in it or when the result is simply missing something.

You're not obligated to put 110 percent into every tattoo, but if two clients pay the same price for your service, why shouldn't they receive the same treatment?

PRACTICE DOESN'T MAKE PERFECT, BUT IT HELPS

You may be convinced that by simply making your tats every week, you can expect to improve over time.

This is true to an extent, but it's primarily untrue, and there's zero guarantee.

> Relax, you're not obligated to do more, but since you're reading this book, I assume you have a desire to improve.

I've met a shocking number of "artists" who simply stop drawing and honing their skills the moment they start tattooing.

It doesn't matter what style you do; a good artist knows that drawing, painting, and all the shadow work is what really transforms you.

If you're spending most of your free time doom scrolling or partying, then it's no surprise you're disappointed with your progress.

Imagine you're an amateur boxer who doesn't do any pad work or cardio once you go pro. You just like to spar during your training camps. It's highly likely you'll spend most of your time face down on the canvas, especially at events.

How about the football player who pisses about at practice and gets shit-faced every weekend? They're called benchwarmers.

In the tattoo world, everyone wants to be great, but if you constantly make excuses for yourself, then I suggest you get comfy in your bed of mediocrity.

If you consciously avoid practice or simply don't believe you need to practice, how can you expect greatness? On top of that, how can you be so impatient for it?

WHOSE SIDE ARE YOU ON?

Most of us know the stress at the beginning of a tattoo or drawing session, especially if we're anxious, tired, or we generally lack confidence in our abilities.

Even if our attitude is positive as we begin, it only takes one little fuck-up and things go south. It would be different if we acted as our own cheerleaders in our minds, but somehow we tend to bully ourselves instead.

The majority of the time, we operate at sub-50 percent of our abilities, so far from our true potential. Yet we're convinced this is a true representation of our skill level.

Most artists roll out of bed, put their clothes on, head for the studio, and start tattooing (after a coffee, a cig, and twenty minutes of fucking around, of course). Once the tattoo is done, it's time to go home and sulk in our misery. Unsatisfied with our results, we spend our evening comparing ourselves to others. We go to bed sad; then we wake up sad and begin tattooing (likely sad) with lower self-esteem than we had the day before.

Doesn't sound like a recipe for success, does it?

DO YOU HAVE A VIRUS?

Most artists I've met (myself included) have an autonomous system installed that essentially acts as their own personal progress blocker.

This system that they're unaware of, and unaware of how to uninstall, is single-handedly working against them every day.

It's generally understood as being "highly critical" or "hard on yourself", but for some people, the roots are much deeper, requiring a lot more than a little word of encouragement to treat it.

We're so familiar with this system being a part of our daily lives that we don't realise it's something we can offload. And when we finally do learn that we can offload it, it's very rare that we're eager to do the heavy lifting.

If you do wish to offload, you'll quickly learn whether you're on your own team.

Naturally, you'd assume that you're your own biggest supporter, but for most of us, we get so battered and bruised along the way that we end up being our own biggest haters.

Convinced that being an asshole to ourselves is actually beneficial, we're only creating more and more dysfunctional internal behaviours, most of which we project all around us.

I'LL HAVE THE CRANIECTOMY, PLEASE

For years I suffered from my impatience. I was completely oblivious to this internal pressure I had adopted to become successful or achieve greatness at such a young age. I'm not sure how or where it came from, but it's still increasingly present in today's world.

Perhaps I romanticised all the greats who succeeded from a young age.

Perhaps it was society's idealistic ways that had poisoned my mind.

I figured it was mostly because of financial and security benefits. More money, less problems, right?

I would compare myself to others on a daily basis. I'd create, compare, suffer, soothe, recover, and repeat.

Every time I burnt out, I'd spend two weeks deep in paralysis and procrastination. I never identified it as a depression, but that became very apparent the more familiar I got with burnout.

Once I'd charged my battery a little, I'd enter the new period with the weight of my previous failures.

I was under this impression that I had to redeem myself and make up for lost (wasted) time.

I also adopted this idea that I was responsible for rescuing my parents from any financial pressure that they had. Or repaying them for the debt they had taken on to provide for my brother and I. My parents weren't getting any younger, and in my own mind, I was letting them down every time I crashed.

All of this, combined with the fact that I refused to work a regular job, was a heavy burden to carry each time I awoke. It was like walking around every day with a bag of bricks that felt increasingly heavier the older I got. I didn't realise I was filling the bag myself, nor was I aware I could put it down.

I resisted at first because it felt selfish to focus entirely on myself. I couldn't abandon this idea that felt important for so long.

When I learnt that I'm no use to anyone if I can't take care of myself, it was a lot easier to take the steps.

WALK BEFORE YOU CAN RUN

It doesn't matter how old you are; if you keep crashing, then you need to slow down.

It doesn't matter how much experience you have; if things aren't making sense, then you need to clear your cache.

Around April 2021, I began therapy and entered an unofficial sick leave from tattooing. After a few sessions with my therapist, I got comfortable with starting from the beginning and moving slowly. I was already capable of so much, but I was biting off more than I could chew.

Some days I'd crawl all day. Some days I'd try to stand up, maybe take a couple of steps. Naturally, some days I ran as fast as I could (because YOLO) and then spent the next day in bed.

The difference this time was that I didn't shame myself for it.

The next time I felt like running, I'd just have to control myself a little better.

Eventually, I learnt that I wanted consistency and that pacing myself was the only way forward.

Of course, this is a metaphor. I didn't have to learn how to walk again. However, constant overstimulation and unpredictable ups and downs had left me feeling defeated.

My therapist suggested that I get tested for ADHD.

Upon thorough investigation, I was diagnosed with ADHD and birthed into a whole new universe of information.

At first, I felt relieved. Everything made sense for a moment. Yet another light turned on in my head and exposed a much bigger mess.

Shortly after, I entered a depression far worse than anything I'd ever experienced in my life. The more I learnt, the more I realised I had so much work to do.

Around a year ago, I began taking prescribed serotonin reuptake inhibitors (antidepressants).

Today, I've never felt more grateful to be alive in my entire life. I'm not ecstatic, but I'm content. I've sustained a peaceful, abundant, creative, and loving year. I've been more consistent this year than the past ten years of adulthood.

Granted, I feel slightly numb at times, but compared to where I was, it's a no-brainer, and I can see myself weaning off of them completely in the near future.

Now, the world has mixed emotions about these meds, I

personally have no medical knowledge, and I'm certainly not recommending them.

However, there are no more surprises. My ADHD doesn't control me. I sleep well. My emotions are regulated. I'm in love with the good and the bad.

Most importantly, I'm patient again, and I love practising everything.

I don't care for moving fast, I just love being.

If any of this resonates with you, please have an open mind and ask for help.

I never considered myself someone who could have ADHD or other issues, simply because I never suffered as badly as other people I knew.

You *will* get there. You *can* be free. You *can* have the life you desire. You just might need a little juice cleanse first.

Topic #11

The Business: The Blind Leading the Blind

The business is the reason I'm here, and it's the reason you're reading this.

It's the reason we make tattoos for a living and have many beautiful experiences and connections.

It's why we have the ability to travel comfortably anywhere in the world.

It's probably the reason you think you're the most interesting kid from your hometown too.

We all know we couldn't sustain this life without it, so I'd like to begin this chapter with a heartfelt thank you to all the humans who got me here.

> My first thank you goes to the owners of the studios I worked for in the past (you know who you are). Because of you, I was moulded into the man I am today. The man I wasn't able to be when I worked for you.
>
> I saw a lot of colours in the industry, and I was able to get my foot in the door thanks to you.
>
> I made a lot of beautiful connections with people who appreciated me for who I was.
>
> I constantly questioned how badly I really wanted to be a tattoo artist because you made things so complicated.
>
> You pushed my limits and showed me there was so much more to me.
>
> I thank you all for the drama you supplied, the doubt and worries, the anxiety, the pressure, the depression, the sleepless nights, the burnouts, the nicotine addiction, the genuine acts of kindness, the fake acts of kindness, the confusion, the laughter, the trickery, and most importantly, the *clarity*. It was a team effort, and as I write this from a place of peace, I cannot take all the credit for being here.

Despite the zesty undertones, I'm genuinely grateful, and I really do appreciate all the effort you've made, and continue to make, that allows most of us to live a happy life.

HOWEVER, like most great things in this life, the corruption and exploitation runs deep. So deep that it's almost an entirely separate business in itself.

I do empathise with the innovators. They just wanted to make our lives easier. I'm sure they never expected humans to do what humans do and ruin *everything* with their insatiable greed and narcissism.

CORRUPTION

Regardless of where you are in your career or what industry you're in, I'm sure you've tasted corruption. It may not have looked and smelled like corruption, but it was still corruption of something once pure.

What I'm saying here is that the tattoo industry is a fucking shitshow.

In my experience, it's been 60/40: 60 percent business and 40 percent tattooing. Sixty percent to the business, and 40 percent to the ones tattooing.

At first I was like, "Okay, sure. That makes perfect sense. The business takes care of the paperwork and all the necessary nonsense I don't wanna think about."

I'm no good with organisation, marketing, or managing myself (or so I was led to believe), so of course, I should pay someone the majority share of my efforts to do the heavy lifting. Sounds fair, right?

The owners had big plans to take over the industry, so the place was constantly evolving. One studio became two, then three, then four, then three again. With employees coming and going, the energy was more unpredictable than the weather, making it nearly impossible for me to settle.

I was very close to the owners in all the studios I worked in, and none of them have been the "sensitive artist" type. More like "wannabe rapper"–type hustlers. Very smart and charismatic people, just not a lot of compassion.

I quickly learnt that having a creative gift and a lot of potential made me a target for extortion.

I moved fast, and within the first two weeks of my apprenticeship, I was tattooing real clients. One month in, and I was told to start expecting cash in hand. Actually, even before then, I was overpromised a bunch of luxurious nonsense.

As you can imagine, my sense of self was suddenly tenuous. My goal was to fit in and keep up, so my precious feelings and emotions were put on the shelf.

At any sign of discomfort, I was offered a quick fix to tide me over.

I was new to living alone, having to take care of my essential human needs. On top of that, I was convinced I could balance a whole new trade. Balance wasn't even something I was aware of at that age. I assumed, "I'm young, so my mind and body will take care of everything by themselves". Obviously, I had no idea my mind and body were keeping track of every little act of neglect and discomfort.

> What does this have to do with "the business"? Well, my friend, you *are* the business.

All of this desperation for comfort and peace makes the business aspect so attractive because it promises freedom and peace of mind. It suggests that all your wildest dreams are possible. Just imagine—especially if you came from less than others—being told you have a chance to gain it all.

Imagine you're a kid in a mall with your parents' credit card. You don't even know what you want. You certainly don't *need* anything in there, yet your brain says, "Fuck that, I *want* everything!"

HUMAN MAGPIES

My bosses and peers loved to romanticise the high life. They pursued shiny things, thinking it would deliver them to a place of power and respect.

It did, momentarily, like it's all designed to do.

As a young gun, I was so enchanted by this idea. It seemed so much better than a simple life of less, and it was almost like there was no in between.

Fortunately, the times that I actually got paid for my efforts, it was never a lot. At the time, I wished there was more, and it caused me a lot of unhappiness.

Now that I'm older, I'm actually glad I never got paid more. I would've only had more to spend on clothes and shallow things in order to make people think I was actually doing well.

See, this is where I learnt about business—in the field. There were no official teachers or seminars. It was every man for himself.

The motto was literally, "Fake it till you make it".

I loved that idea. It was a whole new concept to me. They made it look so simple too. All you had to do was manipulate people (especially yourself and your clients), spend all your earnings on things so you appeared rich, and repeat this system until you actually *were* rich.

Naturally, this system is flawed and completely nonsensical because it was endorsed by lost, soulless children who needed to prove others wrong. Hence the appeal to such children.

OUR FINANCIAL BURDENS

I was very fortunate as a child, but I carried the financial stress of my parents for a good ten years.

Most of my choices and motivation were fuelled entirely by the idea of financial freedom and comfort for my family. Whether we admit it or not, it's what we all want, right?

My theory on why tattoo artists suffer so much in this business is primarily because of this ideology.

Whether you're new or you've been here for ten-plus years, it's likely you have a completely distorted view of reality in this industry.

In my opinion, the majority of artists love shiny things more than they love making tattoos.

I'm not suggesting they're to blame, nor am I suggesting they shouldn't be here. I'm simply saying the influence and encouragement of such an idea is where things get twisted.

And please forgive me if I sound like a boomer. I guess that's who I am now.

The clever business boys have managed to *convince* almost everyone that it's easy to draw and learn how to tattoo. They promote that a short spurt of stress and hard work will earn you a sexy and comfy life.

I'm not saying it's impossible. I'm just saying it's a lot more about repetition, love, and patience over an extensive period of time, and far less about the nonsense they throw in the mix.

But notice I said *convince*. *Collins Dictionary* provides synonyms like *persuade, flatter, entice, allure, encourage, influence, get, prompt, urge, prevail upon*.

In some cases, the word *convince* could mean helping someone believe in themselves, see the "bright side," and realise their potential. But it can also be used to deceive impressionable, genuine, or desperate people.

The business has adopted the latter.

Young adults should not be lost, confused, depressed, overworked, and teased with salvation—not now, not ever. Especially when all we seek is creativity, connection, stability, and warmth.

Humans aren't perfect, yet somehow we'll forever refuse to believe it's not attainable.

The business will tease you that it's just around the corner, every step of the way, robbing you of today's happiness.

The business will keep you loyal to your goal whilst you simultaneously fund theirs.

Don't give them all the credit, though. They're just copying the blueprint society has been feeding us since day one.

Oh, the business.

THE APPLE DOESN'T FALL FAR FROM THE TREE

After a while, the student becomes the master, and the cycle grows stronger. Social media makes it increasingly easier to deceive and benefit from immorality.

In the industry, we love to say, "That's just how it is now", which is essentially just another way of avoiding our responsibility to do better.

Students who adopt "the business" way of life can quickly become lost amongst their influencer friends and their walk-in wardrobes, drowning in the useless shit they hoped would save them.

Some decide to continue working for the boss and pay their 50 percent because it's easier. The rest travel or open their own studio. The *business* is officially their own, and it's time to see what they've learnt.

Usually they'll have a decent clientele already, most of whom are excited to support them. The first months can be successful due to the momentum and excitement, so the future seems bright.

However, if they don't stay on their toes, the idea of losing their precious business will come creeping in.

By this point, they already have a mortgage on their house, a baby or two, and a brand-new BMW. With so much to lose, and their tattoo business being their only source of income, going bankrupt is not an option.

Discomfort and living poor is also not an option, especially once they've tasted how sweet the business can be.

This is where the unethical fuckery begins.

Now the intensity to which the fuckery can manifest solely depends on the quality of the work, multiplied by how soulless the person is.

SHADY TACTICS

Let's paint a picture: you're a client going to XYZ Studios to fulfil your dream of getting your first tattoo.

You're greeted by a very friendly shop manager who offers you a coffee and a comfy seat.

You get to talking, and the manager quotes you a price for your project and gives you a couple of artists to choose from.

Artist A will cost €2000 per session. They're evidently much better, but you can first book a time with them a year from now.

Artist B "usually" costs €1500 per session, but they have an open slot next week, and the manager can offer you a discount.

Regardless of what you choose, imagine you then find out that a friend got tattooed by Artist B last week and only paid €200 for the day because Artist B is still an apprentice.

It must be a mistake! There's no way that lovely manager (who is literally hired to sell you stuff) has lied to you!

Again, it's not a crime, and I'm aware it happens in literally every industry ever, but it's the principle I want you to focus on.

If an artist was making genuinely good tattoos, surely they wouldn't need such aggressive sales tactics, right?

COMING CLEAN

As a tattoo artist yourself, imagine someone manipulating your own family members or friends this way. Would you be mad? But how can you feel mad when you do it to other people's family members? Are they less important to the world?

What gives you the right to believe you can take advantage of people to fund your own life?

How can you exercise your influence and only benefit yourself?

I am 100 percent guilty of all of this behaviour too. I learnt it from the people around me, and it fuelled my lifestyle for years.

Combined with my own pressure to free myself and my family of financial burdens, I was able to justify any wrongdoings because I felt I was entitled to.

I take full responsibility and ownership of my unethical decisions.

To take, take, take and never pay it forward only left me in debt with the laws of nature.

In a fair world, I would have to redeem myself and prove myself worthy for taking advantage of fellow humans simply for financial gain.

I would have my licence revoked as an ill practitioner and a poor representative of the craft.

But this is not a fair world. This is a cruel one, and we continue to pour gas on the fire because there are no consequences for sloppy behaviour and bad manners.

The fuckery goes undetected, for there are no radars, so we walk free, knowing what we have done. And each day we must continue to convince the world that we are whole.

What makes any of us think society stands a chance when we behave this way?

WHAT DOES THIS HAVE TO DO WITH ME?

Well, that depends.

Here are a few things that could help you identify whether or not you're under the influence of "the business".

Before meditating on these questions, it's very helpful to clear your mind first. Being in a neutral state of mind will make it easier to revoke any emotional bias from your reality.

Answer as honestly as you can, and you'll know exactly what it has to do with you.

So, let's get to the bottom of this.

1. Do you genuinely appreciate the craft?
2. Do you express gratitude for all it provides?
3. Do you think you're more important than others?
4. Do you have external pressures that rely on your success?
5. Do you have an insatiable hunger for more?
6. Will you stop at nothing to get what you want?
7. Are you being genuinely supported by your boss/colleagues?
8. Do you have a clear private/work–life balance?
9. Are you experiencing new thoughts or desires for material things?
10. Are you increasingly motivated to work more because of the money?
11. Do your peers gaslight or emotionally manipulate you?
12. Do you have a clear understanding of what's expected of you and how you can achieve your goals through tattooing?
13. Do you only receive praise for your efforts?
14. Do you only receive criticism for your efforts?
15. Do you feel trapped in your current situation?

If necessary, it may help to seek validation from someone who knows your situation on a personal level. It's also likely that some of your peers share the same feelings, and it may be worth opening a discussion.

THINGS YOUR EMPLOYER DOESN'T WANT YOU TO KNOW

If you're genuinely good at your job, you may be led to believe otherwise. Knowing your own value or being overqualified and underappreciated is not profitable for your current employer. They need you to believe that they are the masterminds, and you should not doubt their powers, especially if they're insecure about losing you.

If you're genuinely bad at your job, you may also be led to believe otherwise. A false sense of confidence goes a long way in this industry. Sales and profits rise when an artist can fool everyone into believing they make high-quality tattoos. This may feel great at the beginning, but when the dust settles—and you realise your true abilities are lacking—you'll be quite upset.

If you're codependent for too long, your employer can/will take advantage of you in ways you could never imagine. You'll be a doormat for a long time, and it'll require tremendous courage to stand up.

If you're new to the country you work in, please do your own homework. If you're foreign to the language, don't rely on the company you work for to tell you how it all works. It's very possible they will lie, cheat, and steal for as long as they can until you grow wiser. Also, if the contract has too many pages, find the nearest exit.

Topic #12

Our Dear Clients

Most artists in the industry didn't become tattooists for the customer service. They just want to do their thing, and the customers will get what they get. That's fine.

What's not fine is overcharging and overpromising a high-quality tattoo experience that ends in disappointment and irreversible damage.

What's also not fine is lying, cheating, mistreating, and taking advantage of genuine people who pay their hard-earned money for your time. Genuine people who deserve equal and fair treatment. People who, despite being difficult at times, are family members and loved ones to others.

We all have family and loved ones, blood or not, and we should expect that they're in the best hands when they're getting a tattoo, having their hair cut, or being taken care of in the hospital.

It breaks my heart to imagine my own loved ones paying for a service they're excited for and being taken advantage of for no reason other than autonomous greed and poorly educated people.

I've been guilty of this many times, and for a while I was convinced it was okay. At times, financial stress would influence my decision-making and cause me to overcharge my client. Other times, I wouldn't be taking care of myself, so my client would suffer unnecessarily. I can't count how many times I rescheduled or cancelled clients in the first six years of my career, but it was too many.

Naturally, I began encouraging my peers to adopt the same habits in order to support/justify my own behaviour.

Sometimes clients can annoy us, but it doesn't mean they're annoying people. There's just a poor level of communication, and often we're not able to understand them. It's much easier to blame the client and bitch about them to soothe our egos, especially if we think we're more important.

STORY TIME

In 2021, I worked for a popular studio in Denmark. I took on a project for a client that required a lot of work. Let's call this client John.

John came to me because he wanted his back piece reworked into something he actually liked.

He'd had the original tattoo made over ten years prior. It was unfinished, and unfortunately it wasn't the best experience.

John was very excited to get his new back piece as soon as humanly possible. He worked in an industry where cash was never an issue, so he became popular at the studio. We started his back and it was brand-new after four sessions.

John was happy. The process took longer than expected, but it healed great, and the project was a success.

However, he'd caught the fever—this experience only left him wanting more and more.

Shortly after this project, I stopped working at this studio for mental health reasons.

A few weeks passed, and I caught wind that John had booked multiple sessions at the studio with the owner. Not only that, but they had made him an offer he couldn't refuse. Since he was so anxious to get covered in tattoos, why not let the new apprentice work on his leg at the same time?

"He's much cheaper, and he's really fast, so you'll be covered in no time."

It was settled. John was booked in for multiple sessions whenever he had time. Being self-employed meant he could expedite this process much quicker than the average client.

John was the perfect type of client for this studio—multiple sessions each week, two artists getting paid, two artists with complete freedom. They were benefitting grossly from this situation.

Naturally, John expected to benefit from this exchange as well, as he should.

However, this experience began turning sour when John complained of extreme aches and pains after his sessions. Painful bruising surrounded all the areas. Unusual swelling limited his movement. The bleeding and oozing wouldn't stop, even days later.

"This is normal when you get big projects done. Just relax and you'll be fine in a couple of days."

John's next session was a week later. He was excited to get more work done, but they couldn't continue anything that was unfinished because he was barely 50 percent into the healing process.

Bear in mind, he had two artists working simultaneously on different parts of his body, at the same time.

So they simply started more new pieces and figured they'd just connect everything at different times.

After a short while, his tattoos weren't healing at all. John was working in between all of his sessions and barely took time to rest, which, as you can imagine, doesn't help. On top of this, he was in a constant battle with a nasty flu, which he claimed was very uncommon for him.

Eventually, John went to the emergency room and was told he had a severe infection. He was given antibiotics so his body could recover.

The amount of times John had to have things retouched dragged the process out so long that it was almost as if he'd had everything tattooed twice over. He was constantly in a state of progress, yet nothing ever seemed to be finished.

Despite the doctors' advice, John continued getting tattooed. His artists clearly didn't care much for his health, either, as they continuously assured him he'd be fine.

I'd never seen such an anticlimactic display of craftsmanship in my entire life. To witness this in a so-called professional environment was beyond surreal.

Eventually John had to throw in the towel. He'd endured eight rounds of various antibiotics in one year and barely got to celebrate a finished tattoo. He'd trusted them wholeheartedly to put their expertise to good use and was left disappointed.

After a tough decision to cancel the remainder of his appointments, John was kicked whilst he was already on the ground. He was made to believe it was all his fault—that he simply had "sensitive skin"—and was told that cancelling all of his appointments was a huge inconvenience to the studio.

Now, please bear in mind, this studio claims to be one of the best in Europe, with absurdly high prices, appealing mostly to a clientele with a taste for luxury.

I can't begin to imagine the amount of money the studio gained from John alone, leaving him feeling dissatisfied, guilty, and financially robbed.

Even worse, another client of mine claimed they almost died from blood poisoning days after their sessions. Guess where they got tattooed. Same place as John.

Guess what they were told. "It's likely your fault. We have no idea how this could've happened."

These events ricocheted, causing further damage not only to John and my other client but to others who visited this studio and were tattooed by these artists.

Considering these types of things happened countless times, and with the word-of-mouth spreading like wildfire, the damage multiplied to areas it never should've reached.

All it takes is for one client to share their story, and another client to put two and two together. Have more people been blamed for their "sensitive skin"? Abso-fuckin-lutely. Taken advantage of? You betcha!

When a client has a bad experience at a studio, they commonly name the studio before the artist. Like if your friend gets food poisoning from a pizza place, it doesn't really matter who made the pizza or how it happened. The whole restaurant suffers. Or does your friend just have a sensitive stomach?

So when the truth came out, all of the artists who worked for this studio, past and present, suffered because of the sloppiness of the owner. Even the ones with good intentions. How could they know better if they were taught by a person like this? The owner is a role model for all employees, and if they say something is normal, then it's normal.

The level of distortion caused by this event is a layer cake of shit that even the stomach of a pig couldn't digest.

The conflict begins when the artists know something is wrong but have no voice. It creates a resistance within them that they should never have to deal with. They get so used to avoiding the truth in the workplace that they become a distasteful version of themselves. They have to keep up the facade, treating clients the same way or making them believe the same kind of nonsense.

"The ink just didn't stay so well."

"Do you drink or smoke? That usually makes your tattoo heal badly."

"I know we agreed on a price, but because we did all these extra retouch sessions, you'll have to pay more."

It doesn't matter what they say. The initial response is to blame the client instead of owning up to their sloppiness.

Honestly, people will be people.

But for the ones who truly give a shit and wish to do better, you're very strong, and I commend you for that. It took me a long time to identify and unlearn a lot of the dysfunctional traits within myself.

When you tattoo so many clients over the years, it's understandable that you can eventually take them for granted. You assume there will be an endless supply for your whole career, the same way we just assume there will always be needles and ink.

NOW WHAT?

If you're not guilty of mistreating your clients, at least evaluate how well you do treat them. There may be room for improvement.

If you pride yourself on being above your clients, speak to a therapist.

If you're no stranger to being shitty at times, welcome to the club. We can all be imperfect humans together.

Start by trying to identify these things in your life:

- **Your workload:** How many clients each day? How many days each week? Are you overwhelmed by your workload? Could you work a little less or a little slower?
- **Your clientele:** Older, younger, male, female, etc.
- **Gratitude:** Do you express gratitude daily for every meal? For a good night's sleep? For clean water?
- **Authenticity:** When you say, "Thank you", "I'm so grateful", or "I appreciate you", is it genuine? Or is it just an automatic response?

Find a new way to express gratitude that will snap you out of your autonomic responses.

I'm a firm believer that gratitude is the expressway to a kinder life.

You don't have to train or pay for it. You can start right this moment. Here are some questions for you:

- Where are you right now?
- Are you warm or cold?
- Can you smell anything?
- What noises can you hear?
- Is your heart beating fast or slow?
- Do you feel safe?
- Did you eat and drink recently?
- How's your breath (not the smell)?
- Is it light or dark outside?

- When did you last speak to loved ones?

Select one of these subjects, and express a little gratitude for it.

Carry your gratitude like you carry your smartphone, and give thanks to each moment like you give your attention to strangers online.

Express gratitude even for the moments you'd consider not so good. There's always something precious in there.

The weather isn't shit; your mentality is.

Your client isn't annoying; your mentality is.

You reap what you sow.

You attract what you believe you deserve.

Take responsibility for yourself. Your clients shouldn't pay the price for your dysfunction.

Train hard to alter your perspective, and you will learn to show grace unconditionally.

Topic #13

The Chain of Influence

One of the most dangerous forces in today's world is influence. Most of us are so preoccupied with how we appear from the outside that we're oblivious to when, if, how, and why we're influencing others or being influenced ourselves.

In my year of reflection, I distanced myself from contributing to social media to spend time on the sidelines. I tried to free myself of assumptions and prejudice so I could reflect without projecting my own issues.

You'd think it would be difficult to understand people's intentions on social media, but it seems to boil down to a few similar ones:

1. To share things they create and indulge the illusion of community
2. To monetize from their every move so they can become their own boss
3. To create and identify with a version of themselves they prefer

Influence is a powerful currency in 2024, and we all have a price we'd settle for.

THE INFLUENCERS

These days, anyone can be influential; it just depends how the audience perceives them. The more confident you are, the more success you have, the more desirable your life is, the more influential you'll be.

Look at the people on the TV shows about tattooing; the majority of them are absolute dog shit at tattooing, and they represent the craft poorly, yet somehow they're considered good on TV.

In simple terms, to influence is to persuade. To persuade is to get someone to agree to something you idealise.

Now, if you're good at what you do, you can naturally influence someone without force.

If you're not quite so good yet, you can still forcefully influence someone.

If you're really clever, you can forcefully influence someone in a way that feels natural, regardless of your abilities to tattoo.

Most don't even realise how influential they are or how much responsibility they carry as influencers of the industry.

Imagine you follow someone online, their artwork looks alright, their political stance is nonsense, they're honestly kind of a shit person, but they post decent memes, and you find them attractive.

If you're unsure of what a good tattoo is, you'll likely believe whatever they show you.

If this person is attractive to you, you'll likely be blinded by that entirely.

Modern society makes it so apparent for us to see who's an influencer. (Hint: they usually have a little tick next to their username and wear sunglasses 24/7.)

In the real world, most people who are verified online walk around like they're verified in real life (even if they pay for it).

My issue with this is that most people feel like they're entitled to this position because they have "earned it" through experience.

Now this would be valid if there was a certifiable educational system in place, but there isn't. In some cases, a person's portfolio is enough and the work speaks for itself.

If you only tattoo in front of a handful of people and no credible sources can vouch for your actual abilities, then how can you be so influential? In a perfect world, this wouldn't be possible if everyone's heads were screwed on right, but I'll remind you, this is not a perfect world.

The shortcuts and life hacks that are accessible to the average Joe only make things a mess.

In our world, someone can be tattooing for one to two years, get a decent camera, take great pictures of their below-average work, edit said pictures to look like the tattoos are impressive, post online, and instantaneously convince a multitude of people worldwide.

Distortion of our industry is progressing at such a disturbing rate, especially with AI and the fact that people's minds are becoming so desensitised to what's real, and they justify the use of technologies that make the process less intimate.

We're so comfortable with abusing these amenities to our benefit that no one wants to be the one to piss on the bonfire.

I've met many artists who are so far gone that they prefer to identify with their online identity rather than the one they were born with.

I'm sure we've all experienced it—you finally see someone's artwork up close, and it's disappointing. Not because you had high expectations but because their online depictions are so far from the truth that it breaks your heart.

Most times we still don't have the strength to be honest. We certainly can't tell the truth in person. The client will be like, "What do you mean it's shit?" and the artist will say, "Wow, bro, thanks".

And even if you do decide to be more honest, the artist will be like, "Wow, so you've never been honest before?" and the relationship crumbles.

This works both ways. What if you're actually terrible at making tattoos but everyone around you is so programmed to sugarcoat everything to keep you happy? How would that make you feel?

The longer we avoid the truth, the longer we distort reality.

In the meantime, people are still being influenced by fakes, being taught how to follow suit, naturally leading the confident ones to influence and continue in their master's footsteps.

THE INFLUENCED

The tattoo industry can be ruthless for apprentices. If you're not a "pushover" then you're "cocky" and "entitled". Sounds toxic already, doesn't it?

I understand there has to be some respect for the hierarchy of experience, but some people take it too far.

A lot of unhealed children are currently in positions of power, "teaching" the next generation of humans about life as a tattoo artist.

Now, the *influenced* aren't just apprentices; they can also be experienced tattoo artists that haven't managed to reach independence yet.

This isn't news to many of you, since it's so common in the real world to be divided into wolves and sheep.

The tattoo industry has somehow adopted this same system in order to keep the wolves satisfied.

To keep it simple, if you believe you're a sheep, you will remain a sheep for as long as you believe so. You will survive on whatever the wolves give you and remain inside your little sheep house (or whatever sheep reside in).

Granted, not all have been raised or encouraged to have a strong support system within themselves, and often they are prey for the wolves.

Once a wolf knows you have sheep tendencies, it's their natural instinct to manipulate and keep you where they want you.

I don't know much about psychology, and I'm not academically educated, but I've experienced my fair share of sociopathic and manipulative behaviour over the past ten years.

Some of the worst tattoo artists I've met have been master manipulators. They single-handedly conjured a following of loyal sheep that claimed to believe they were the greatest source of information.

It gets to a point where the influenced are so strung out that they endlessly run in circles looking for answers, doubting their own abilities and running into walls each week, wondering why things don't make sense.

These same people are the ones who work tirelessly day and night and pay 40–60 percent of their entire monthly earnings to this masterful wolf.

They're brainwashed and limited to what they experience

because their wolf prides themselves in notoriously gatekeeping their knowledge and projecting themselves higher and higher throughout time.

Sheep wouldn't dare question the methods of their master for they don't favour the outcome.

Such methods would be admirable if they actually helped the sheep, but they simply keep the rent paid.

The sheep can go to market and attain knowledge from other masters, but if they bring it home and the master finds out, they will be quickly shunned because the idea of a sheep developing beyond the skills of their own master is unspeakable. Outshining or praising knowledge from someone other than their own master is punishable by death for an honest sheep.

> This, of course, is not the case for some studios. I can only speak for the ones I know of. The fact that the vast majority of studios I know have operated this way gives me a reason to believe it's a common pattern in the industry.

Some sheep aren't bound to a master. They rely solely on the methods of online wolves.

Thanks to the dishonesty and quality distortion online, some sheep never understand what true quality is. They live in a state of limbo, hoping that someone will show them greatness, but they've never seen a tattoo in real life that matches the ones they see online.

THE UNTAMED POWER OF INFLUENCE

Now you have an idea of the game, you can imagine how the wolves can get addicted to power.

Unhealed children finally have a sense of control over weaker humans who remind them of themselves. They get so comfortable with their sense of importance that living without it is not an option. It's a lot easier than figuring out how to develop and grow with the times, and for a lot of wolves, they can retire a lot earlier when a bunch of sheep pay their bills.

There's an incentive to make more space in a studio just so they can hire more sheep. It doesn't take long to train a sheep to start making money for you, so the more the merrier. You can just make the older sheep train the babies and do all the hard work for you. You won't even have to reward them; you'll just feed them a false sense of responsibility, and they'll eat it right up!

It's even more effective if the sheep believe they're working for a really good studio. They'll be loyal for a very long time.

To make things worse, if these sheep ever summon the strength to leave and work independently, they'll only encounter a whole new world of issues.

They'll only be able to communicate in the language they've learnt from their evil master and wonder why no one understands them.

"I was under the impression I was really good at my old place. Why am I suffering more now?"

The sheep will either return to what's familiar or start from the beginning again.

I'm not suggesting they wasted time, but if they have to unlearn a bunch of bad habits and learn better world-proof behaviours, then it's quite inconvenient as an adult with responsibilities. It certainly wasn't in the contract, was it?

Some famous tattoo artists, often shop owners and very often sociopaths, have been known to make life exceedingly difficult for artists who have "crossed them", exercising their power to essentially prohibit artists from doing business with anyone of their choosing.

Just as spoilt children throw pity parties, spoilt tattoo artists will do the same. If you no longer wish to work for them, you can totally expect them to make life difficult for you.

THE DESIRE TO BE INFLUENTIAL

Welcome to the modern world, where it's sexy to be influential.

As long as it looks and sounds like you're intelligent or credible, it doesn't matter if you actually are! People are so naive they'll swallow whatever shit-filled spoon you feed them!

As I said before, this appeals to the unhealed child, the university dropouts, the weak and confused, and the impatient.

I've had a handful of followers in my career so far, both online and in person.

I had an apprentice before I was old enough to know what to do with one. I was given responsibilities I wasn't qualified to handle.

I've seen how poor leadership led to poor behaviours in others.

I've witnessed all the laziness and entitlement from poorly raised apprentices.

I've seen poorly educated yet confident apprentices give advice to newer apprentices.

It's so desirable to be influential because deep down, people just want to be helpful. They're not all bad. They never meant to be. They just learnt this behaviour.

Why shouldn't we all want to be helpful? It's what makes humanity thrive.

But like I explained in the last chapter, we can't help anyone until we truly help ourselves. Once that's done, perhaps try to teach by being a great example. Influence naturally like the greats did.

There's no need to force-feed or appear great when you're at peace with your inner child.

There's a reason the loudest in the room are the ones who suffer the most in silence—they have a lot to compensate for.

If you were content with your abilities, would you belittle others to prop yourself higher?

THE LACK OF RESPECT

Perhaps it's a Western thing. Perhaps it's an atheist thing or a Gen-Z coping mechanism.

Regardless, the one thing most artists have in common is their lack of respect for literally everything.

I had to learn respect myself. It's something I'm still learning, especially in the industry.

It's hard when you're surrounded by people who don't respect themselves or anything they acquire. It gives us a taste of endless futility.

I mean, our industry contributes to a decent portion of one-time-use plastics and other materials in order to make a tattoo (a nonessential human privilege).

This behaviour of constantly throwing away and not being able to make the most of things to their full capacity, is what—I believe—to be partly responsible for how we end up treating everything.

I mean, with the sheer volume of things, it's tough to value everything each time we work.

We simply suck things dry, and we only want to pay the bare minimum for it, because we need so many things in order to do what we do.

Eventually we don't differentiate between inks, needles, or people.

Clients come and go, friends and peers come and go, someone we work with for five years can suddenly move away, and we move on. Social media has an endless thread of knowledge or people we can fill the holes with, so we never experience loss in a traditional sense.

We forgot to respect and honour each moment with something, so we have nothing to miss.

The heartbreaking thing is that some of the most beautiful and exciting people I've ever met have worked in the tattoo industry, they just weren't capable of being appreciated or showing appreciation.

In the most recent years, I've seen less and less of these people and experienced a whole new wave of degenerate inbred piranhas, longing for anything to chew on, caring only for themselves.

It's almost like the pure ones were defeated or turned sour. Maybe they just moved to the countryside. Who knows.

Topic #14

Money, Money, Money

You know how money affects your life. You know how it affects your judgement. You know how it influences your decisions. How it applies pressure, and how it eases it too. When it brings joy, and when it brings pain.

How you can have more than ever, yet never enough.

You complain you don't earn enough, yet you still get up and work for it.

At times, you may even think you're so important that you should be paid more than doctors.

Once upon a time, I personally believed I could earn a million euros a year making tattoos. I'm sure I could've, but at what cost?

How many people would I have to convince I was worth it?

How many fingers would I work to the bone?

How many days would I be free to enjoy the lifestyle I'm constantly chasing?

How valuable would that million truly be if I had no time to spend it?

Even if there was time, who would I spend it with? Where would I go?

Would I feel proud of myself knowing I'd captured €1 million of hard-earned money for making a bunch of average tattoos?

How about if I knew I had to pay €500,000 in taxes?

Think of all the bills and expenses. All the things I'd buy, simply to cope with the stress of being so busy.

You've already forgotten about what this book is for, haven't you?

I'll remind you: it's about finding clarity so you can be a better human, and ultimately, a better tattoo artist.

A healthier, more colourful version of you.

One that enjoys every day you get to breathe and create, regardless of external factors.

It doesn't mean you can't think about money. Money is something that connects us all. It's the only universal language we all speak. Living without it is not an option, yet it will destroy us all if we get too close.

Modern-day atrocities and genocides are born from greed, and today we all suffer in ways we never should've had to.

The root cause of evil is this twisted fetish we have for possession and control—it's undeniable. Possession of land, money, and the minds of people is the ultimate power.

Maybe I sound like a crazy person to you, but please humour me for a minute.

What makes any of us better than the next if we continue to take more than we need?

We all saw what happened during COVID-19 with the unexpected toilet paper shortage. The overall circulation was eaten up by greed—not fear that you couldn't wipe your ass for another week. Just greed. A fundamental lack of respect for anyone else but yourself.

Your pantry is stocked full of enough things to keep *you* alive for a year, but your neighbour dies after a month.

No one wins.

Now, forgive me for comparing these issues to that of the industry, but perspective is essential.

Some people seem to think that being a tattoo artist makes them exempt from displaying essential human values. I'm not suggesting that you must be a perfect human, but I do believe you'll be happier if you lift your head up and expand your consciousness beyond yourself.

PRICING AND VALUING YOUR WORK

Something we're all familiar with is struggling to price our own time and energy. On top of that, we must maintain our income and survive the waves of our forever-volatile economy.

Naturally, something a human makes with their bare hands is a difficult thing to put a price on.

In the art world, they say that the true value of an artwork is whatever the buyer pays for it. This can be true, but it's difficult to apply to the art of a tattoo artist.

Depending on your style, you're essentially creating something unique every time. If you're not, then it's probably a lot easier to price your work based on the hours you spend creating.

The amount you charge per hour can be conjured based on the amount of experience you have, your originality, your efficiency, your professionalism, your craftsmanship, the quality of the tattoo once it's healed, the rate of customer satisfaction, and the overall consistency of your services. All of this can then be refined relative to your environment, fair market values, supply expenses, rent, taxes, and whatever else is essential for you to remain in business.

It shouldn't be valued based on your social media popularity or what your ego thinks you're worth, especially if your ego and popularity grow.

If you're a hustler, let me remind you that the original purpose of a business is to provide a service within the means of the area it's located within, serving as a functional part of the entire ecosystem. It's not to suck the area dry and leave it behind.

To contribute to this unregulated capitalism for our own gain is to willingly contribute to the suffering of everyone else.

For a human at peace, sustainability is enough.

For a human with an insatiable hunger, nothing is enough.

THINK LONG TERM

I know it's tough, especially in times like these. When the bare necessities are twice the price, we're often left with no choice but to increase our own prices or work more.

This is where I believe humans add to the suffering. It's a chain reaction in which no one wants to suffer, causing everyone to suffer more.

We cannot continue to raise our prices whenever things get tough. Fear of loss cannot be an operating factor for our own self-worth.

It's time that we commit to our own internal compass and rely on that for guidance.

Before we can continue moving forward, we must clarify the negative forces and render them powerless.

Here are some questions that could help you detect the source of your destructive tendencies:

1. Am I consciously influenced by external stressors?
2. Do I follow the crowd and do what others advise me to do?
3. Do I spend a lot of money on liabilities and personal luxuries to strengthen a false sense of identity?
4. Am I motivated by money for shallow reasons?
5. Does the idea of growth and success fuel my efforts as a tattooist more than genuine interest?
6. Am I currently satisfied with all that I am and all that I have?

Once I personally cleared the field for myself, it became increasingly easier to focus on what I valued in my life. My new mentality at the beginning of each month was to pay my bills, set aside some cash for food, and express gratitude for the four weeks of freedom I had secured myself.

There were no more ridiculous goals like "save €10,000 this month" or "make fourteen paintings, document it all, and post content". My focus was more like "water your own plants first", "take a nap if you need one", "be mindful of your consumption", and "if you end up homeless, so be it".

If I was planning my calendar, I would make sure to plot in rest days or reminders to take it slow after a day that I knew would be tiresome. Considering my energy for tomorrow and the day after would allow me to ration my energy for today, and ultimately prevent me from sabotaging the entire week.

I can highly recommend it.

SOMETHING TO CHEW ON

It's always been normal to look the part. Doctors wear their scrubs. The police wear their uniforms. Construction workers wear their protective gear. The Wall Street wank-stains wear their fancy suits.

Tattoo artists were never assigned a special outfit, so we took it upon ourselves to create our own class system.

Since it's become increasingly popular to compensate with your appearance, a lot of people have introduced high-end clothing and gadgets into the equation.

I don't need to describe it to you. It's highly likely you already know.

So, I'll just say this.

Just because you like to look fancy doesn't mean you get to charge more for your work.

Just because you like to buy the latest things doesn't mean your clients should pay more.

Just because you want a better life for yourself doesn't mean you can justify cutting corners.

Oh, and just because you have things you paid a lot of money for doesn't mean you're automatically a more valuable person.

I get it—you are your brand. But if you don't draw the line between work and personal, how can you make sure your personal needs don't affect the way you do business?

Just because your client paid you €3000 for a tattoo doesn't mean it was worth it. It just means you succeeded in convincing them it would be.

If you never checked in with them later down the road and invited them to be honest, how do you know how they really feel about the experience?

You also know what it's like to pay too much for something, but you convince yourself that it's worth it because it's easier than accepting your poor choices.

GOING ON TOUR

If you travel a lot, you'll understand that the price of tattoos varies based on multiple things: the artist, the exclusivity, the shop, the city, the country, the availability, and the popularity of all things combined.

Being a guest artist can appeal to many people for many reasons:

1. The cash.
2. The experience.
3. The dirty, dirty cash.
4. The perspective it offers.
5. That sweet Johnny Cash.
6. Planes are cool.

I have nothing against travelling artists, especially if you're incredible, and it's tough/illegal in your home country. It just bothers me when artists go on tour just to make money and take the spotlight, especially while operating in a toxic manner.

Some people tattoo for one or two years and begin thinking they qualify for guesting. This can be true in rare cases, but in a lot of cases, it's a disaster.

Many of them can't get clients, and if they do, they're often anxious and uncomfortable in unpredictable environments. Therefore, they operate in a flaky survival state instead of a natural one that allows their abilities to flourish. This leaves barely any energy to even consider the well-being of the resident artists and clients who offer their hospitality.

When many of the essential requirements for optimal human conditions aren't met, we struggle to complete the majority of our everyday tasks, let alone provide a quality service. So if we can barely do that in our own comfortable home environment, what makes us so sure we can do it in a brand- new place?

It takes an experienced and weathered tattoo artist to be able to bounce around and provide an incredible service whilst keeping all of their integrity and values intact. That experience is what almost guarantees this artist will actually benefit the environment they visit and not just take from it. Bouncing from city to city, filling your pockets with cash, making average tattoos, and being an inconsiderate leech is something that benefits you, and you only.

At this point, I'm sure it sounds like I'm no fun at parties. I beg to differ. I'm simply trying to shine light on the carelessness of travelling and that our hunger for money and value motivates us to travel far before we're qualified to do so.

Similar to tourism, residents of the world visit each other's countries and leave the country in a worse state than it was before they arrived. It feels quite rare that a person actually visits a new tattoo studio and respects it entirely.

TRUST THE UNIVERSE

This is the part where I may lose a few of you.

This idea abides by the principles of "wu-wei" or "amor fati," the idea of accepting one's fate or going with the flow.

Imagine yourself being one of the two local tattoo artists in your area. The other is the new guy who rented the space directly across the street. Seemingly, he wishes not to join forces, for he has his very own vision. For the sake of the story, let's call him Brian.

At first it seems like nothing has changed. Perhaps there is enough business for the both of you.

Summer arrives and business is slowing down, and what's this? It appears that Brian is gaining popularity. His methods and abilities seem to come naturally. He is always smiling. He never loses his composure, even on quiet days. *What is this sorcery?*

Naturally, the locals have grown fond of his view of the craft. It feels new and exciting.

In fact, last Monday, a potential client was waiting for you to finish your phone call and just happened to gaze across the street. There she saw Brian hovering in his atelier. She claimed that "he literally even levitated at one point" and then winked at her.

Anyway, the details don't matter. The clients can literally smell a better pizza from across the street, and you know that pizza's delicious too.

So you always have options, but what are you gonna do?

Are you gonna begin to resent Brian and have a little pity party in your empty studio?

You've already tried discounting your prices, but now your clientele just think you're desperate. They're certainly not gonna pay a fair price now when the price was 50 percent cheaper last week.

Maybe buying cool clothes will convince the locals you're back on top. Perhaps get one of those inflatable dancing guys you see at car dealerships. That'll get them.

Alternatively, you could just surrender to the laws of nature.

I'm not suggesting you give up, but if you can't keep your business running with your natural abilities, then your only options are to play dirty, right?

If you're resorting to anything that breaches your own personal values and capabilities, then that's beyond natural.

If you're becoming a pest, desperate for clients and business, then that's the feeling everyone else will get.

If your thoughts become bitter, negative, and pessimistic, then that's how your reality will be.

Sure, get a loan, buy more time, but that might result in you bleeding out for longer.

Even your most loyal client, "wee Danny", has started talking about Brian.

You've kicked the can for a while now, and you're a sight for sore eyes.

You can't remember the last time you enjoyed making a tattoo because you've been so focused on the money.

You *could* always just surrender. You *could* just call it a day and be happy for all that you've experienced.

No one said you're giving up, but surrendering to the laws of the universe is a proud and elegant decision not many wish to make.

It's like the art of knowing when you've had enough.

It's leaving the club before the lights come on.

Leaving the table before you overindulge and suffer a bellyache.

Even for the ones who work for someone else, if it just doesn't seem to be working out, you're miserable, and your wage doesn't numb the pain, why not let go of your pride and dare to turn the page?

You can continue in misery, or you can walk another route and see new flowers.

Regardless of how old you are, you can always hang your hat up for a moment to give your soul a break.

Even if it means you have to go back to work in the grocery store, at least you can breathe and see clearly for a while.

Even if you feel defeated, you could always find peace in

knowing you had a good run, and that Brian is taking better care of the locals.

Running a good business shouldn't be about how clever you are or how much money you make (and it certainly isn't about how long you can avoid the tax man). It should be about how honest you are at running that business with all that you're naturally capable of.

If you carelessly break and bend all the rules, defy human rights, and make a mess, it's only a matter of time before nature takes over.

A resistance to the laws of nature is where corruption is born.

Corruption is where mould begins to paint the walls. Greed and ugliness have no place in the industry.

Why force it? Perhaps it wasn't meant to be.

You can't hold on to what once was or what could be because they do not exist today. Open your eyes and surrender to your present situation.

You may be a creative person, but you are not *the* creator.

Just as *Devil's Snare* tightens the more you resist, the universe will eat you alive the more you fight it.

Topic #15

Amateur to Professional

This is where all your hard work must come together if you wish to transform.

Not all desire the pursuit of becoming a professional, and you're about to find out why *I* believe that's a jolly good idea.

I heavily pursued the idea of "going pro" as an artist from the age of sixteen. At twenty-six, I realised I was pursuing it for all the wrong reasons.

I also realised I had no idea what "going pro" even meant or why it was so desirable.

Does success equal professionalism?

Does professionalism equal success?

There's clearly a correlation, but I no longer believe they're reliant upon each other.

We all assume that more "success" requires more responsibility, thus more time spent, more energy out, and as a result, less time remaining to enjoy the fruits of our labour.

Why the fuck is that so desirable?

At this point, it seems pretty clear that more "success" only catapults us further into a pit of despair.

If you don't love the stress and responsibilities of operating at your current level, then I highly doubt you'll love them when you operate at a higher level.

Nonetheless, if you're more of the irrational, gun-slingin', "fuck around and find out" type of player, then yee-hawwww, 'cause I've got some golden nuggies for ya.

SO YOU WANNA GO PRO, HUH?

First of all, I suggest you conjure up a plan.

And by "plan", I don't mean study the law of attraction and make a list of your goals.

I mean a long-term plan that will encourage you to move slow and steady, focusing on consistency, maintaining balance, and progressing at a natural, healthy rate.

Be realistic, not ambitious.

If you wanna grind yourself into someone you're not, simply close this book and start watching senseless motivational shit on YouTube.

I know your brain likes to move fast, but high-speed driving gets you killed, even if you're a good driver.

Avoid shortcuts at all costs. You don't need to ask successful artists for help, nor do you need to hurry up and get smarter.

Has no one told you you're allowed to accept where you are today?

If you want to be yourself when you get there, you can't leave yourself behind.

Stop scheming, planning, and bullshitting.

Surrender to your actual reality.

You've gotta be pretty good at walking before you try running, right?

Experience is what makes us evolve, not buying new gadgets and trying harder each day. Trial and error builds character. Taking your setbacks on the chin and moving forward throughout time is what will deliver you to a prosperous future.

Don't be afraid to grow curious, to get weird and messy, or to venture into the dark and wish you never had.

Forever calculating the right move, avoiding the unknown, and fighting for control will only hold you captive as a prisoner in your own mind, where you're also the guards, the nurse, and the rats between the walls.

WHAT IS A "PRO", ANYWAY?

In my opinion, a professional is someone who rarely gets lost, and when they do, they're quickly back on the road again (without anger or blaming the GPS). They're consistent, reliable, disciplined, independent, and healthy.

Being a pro doesn't mean being a leader, nor does it justify being an asshole.

Making lots of money and having expensive things is *not* what makes you a professional.

Who you associate with is certainly *not* what makes you a professional.

Where you live and work is *not* what makes you a professional.

Doing what you say you'll do every.single.time is what makes you a professional.

Satisfying customers and delivering the experience that you're paid to provide without whining is what makes you a professional.

Taking responsibility for everything you do, especially the failures, is what makes you a professional.

Your ability to be selfless and helpful, accepting of each moment, knowing when to surrender, loving effortlessly, being predictable yet never dull, fearless yet rational, gentle but firm, all while being free of judgement or complaint, is what makes you a professional.

Seeking praise and approval is unnecessary because a professional is exactly where they're supposed to be at all times.

A professional will run the inner workings of their being with grace and humility, tending to each plant in their garden as if it were the only one.

Knowing that they are "professional" means nothing to them because they know no different.

If years go by and you notice this is who you've become, then perhaps you have graduated.

Until you stop forcing it, you will remain as you are.

For the time being, you'll only be a pro at putting your clown suit on and painting your face.

You'll be immune to imposter syndrome because you will simply *be* an imposter.

To "go pro" is to evolve naturally.

A caterpillar cannot force metamorphosis. It cannot transform until its duties as a caterpillar are done.

Becoming a butterfly is not the result of pressure, shortcuts, and pretending. If a caterpillar spent all its energy trying to fly, it would simply die trying.

Breathe... It's not that deep.

Acknowledgments

First of all, I'd like to thank Jack Ede (me) for finally getting your head out of your ass and dealing with your own issues over the past couple years. Writing, funding, and publishing this book from start to finish over the course of twelve months is a monumental achievement for you, and I know you'll avoid giving yourself credit. You were consistent, patient, and resilient, all while sharing your love and kindness for all around you. So well done, honestly.

Thank you to the love of my life and illustrator of this book, Giulia Franck. Thank you for making sure I stayed hydrated, well fed, and well rested when I had busy weeks. You are my rock, and I'm eternally grateful.

Thanks to all the special souls at Scribe for making this entire process so stimulating. Your enthusiasm and expertise kept me fuelled through every stage, and I'm certain this book wouldn't exist without your magic.

Thank you to my previous employers and coworkers for your hospitality and kindness. You all welcomed me with open arms, and I wouldn't be the man I am today without your efforts. Every meal, every lesson, and every opportunity you provided was deeply appreciated.

Thank you to my closest friends: Mitch, Pascal, Karolina, Jesper, Jeppe, Chay, Camilla, and Nanna for your genuine warmth. We may not be as close as we once were, but our connections throughout the years have made my life feel very special thus far.

A heartfelt thanks to every client who has trusted me with their skin and allowed me to continue this beautiful life I lead each day. To choose me when you could choose anyone else is something I value deeply. You've all taught me more than any teacher, without even trying.

Thank you to my family for loving and supporting me relentlessly since day one. Thank you for having my back throughout every endeavour and cooperating when I chose to rebuild my foundations. It's been a team effort, always.

And finally, thanks to the soul reading this book. I appreciate your efforts no matter what they are, even if you don't believe they're enough. I appreciate you showing up for yourself and your people, especially on the days when it's tough. Thank you for never giving up on us and everything you believe in. It's all you.

About the Author

JACK EDE is a Scotland-born artist with an undeniable knack for the creative arts. Now residing in Denmark, Jack has spent the better part of the last decade mastering the intricacies of tattooing, painting, and drawing. Despite forgoing traditional education and art school, his self-taught skills have flourished, enabling him to carve out a successful career as a self-employed artist since 2014. Jack's journey towards the present day has been nothing short of inspiring.

Outside of his professional life, Jack is a fervent explorer of human nature and a proponent of living life at a sustainable pace. His hobbies, ranging from bowling to taking naps, alongside his love for creating with his hands, are a clear reflection of his philosophy. Jack's narrative is one of honesty, encouragement, and validation, offering an honest perspective on life and art.

His upcoming book, *It's Not That Deep: The Essential Workbook for Simplifying Your Life as a Tattoo Artist*, reflects his profound experience and growth within the tattoo community. The book stands as a testament to his dedication, aiming to guide aspiring and current tattoo artists through the mental health challenges and dysfunctional aspects of the industry. Jack's gentle, patient, and compassionate approach to both art and life shines through his work, making him not just an artist but a mentor to many.

www.ingramcontent.com/pod-product-compliance
Lightning Source LLC
Chambersburg PA
CBHW060528080526
44586CB00012B/665